WATER

I would like to thank the company Dalekovod d.d. Zagreb, Croatian Olympic Committee, Split Sports Federation and Split-Dalmatian county — Administrative division for education, culture and sports, who have financially supported the issuing of this book and therefore enabled its formation.

Equally helpful was support from the solleagues who have helped with their ideas, thoughts and knowledge, espesially Prof. Vinko Lozovina, Ph.D.

Finally, I would like to thank all the people who have taken part in professional, linguistic, illustrative and graphical making of the book.

Author

Published by the author

Managing Editor:
Zoran Kačić, B.Sc.

Reviewer:
Prof. Vinko Lozovina, Ph.D.

Translated:
Tomaž Lasič

Photography:
Duje Klarić

Arrangement and printing:
GIPA, Zagreb

First impression of 600 copies

CIP - Cataloguing in publication
LIBRARY OF UNIVERSITY SPLIT

UDK 797.253

Kačić, Zoran
Water Polo Goalkeeper / Zoran Kačić ; <translated Tomaž Lasič ;
photography Duje Klarić>. - Split : published by the author, 2007.

Bibliography.

ISBN 978-953-95690-2-8

I. Water Polo

120803094

ZORAN KAČIĆ

WATER POLO GOALKEEPER

SPLIT 2007.

PREFACE

Talking about goalkeepers means talking about an unique, unusual, but above all a wonderfully perfumed flower. It is their distinctiveness that makes them rare, unpredictable and sets them apart.

The distinctiveness of water polo goalkeeping is determined by its surrounding in the medium of water. Natural giftedness and ease in conquering resistance, friction and gravitation differs and is determined by many factors (eg. physical build, levels of fat around the body). Apart from the motivational and appropriate osteo-muscular factors, buoyancy is a very important and particularly valued quality we should consider in selecting young goalkeepers.

The distinctiveness of a goalkeeping position in any sport assumes a particular approach and specific methods, particularly when dealing with juniors. This is because junior goalkeepers are often relatively lonely and quite rare. That is why we must approach working with such children with great responsibility, firstly as pedagogues and then as coaches. If we do so, these children's' abilities will, with specialist goalkeeping education, gradually grow and in the process reject bad habits and accept and develop correct and positive habits. Certainly, coaches-goalkeepers, who have paid their triumphs and defeats with sweat and tears, can only provide this type of tutelage. That is why only goalkeepers can truly understand and appreciate *the magical dance of a goalkeeper in goals*. To everyone else, including the best coaches, this will remain an unrealised mystery. The conclusion is obvious: Only a goalkeeper to coach goalkeepers!

In the game of water polo, this beautiful "*art of power and spirit*", a goalkeeper stands at its most sensitive if not the most responsible position. The most sensitive because of the difficulty and the beauty of the challenge, most responsible because of the delicacy, importance and direct influence on the final score. As the backbone of the defence, the goalkeeper prevents the opposition from scoring a goal, corrects the mistakes made by the field players with his saves, leaves the area in front of the goal if needed, participates in the struggle for the ball and is frequently involved in structuring the attack and the list could go on. A goalkeeper with such a profile would completely satisfy the requirements and the demands of modern water polo. I do not feel it necessary to point out that the combination of the team making up for goalkeeper's mistakes is for any, even the best team, and the most disappointing feature.

With a few of these general thoughts we welcome and present Zoran Kacic's book-handbook *Goalkeeper in Water Polo*. Conceptualised and realised by an exemplary athlete and an experienced, greatly successful goalkeeper, the book represents a unique event in Croatian sport. Unique in respect that publication of expert literature about water polo is very rare at home and around the world. Its publishing gains even greater importance considering the success that a number of Croatian players and teams have enjoyed for many years.

If it correct to assume that theory makes practice perfect (and vice versa!), the approach and the methodical manner in which this material is presented have become Condicio sine qua non of the modern education of coaches and goalkeepers. In the absence of similar expert reading, Kacic's book is a true sporting gift and a great contribution to training of aspiring young water polo goalkeepers.

dr. Petar Rossi

CONTENTS

1. Introduction — 9
2. Choosing a goalkeeper — 11
3. Basic theoretical premises and calculations of optimal reach — 13
4. Physical preparation of a goalkeeper — 17
    A. Introduction — 17
    B. Dry land training — 19
    C. Water training — 21
        1. General swimming training for goalkeepers — 22
        2. Specific goalkeeping training — 23
            I. Exercises without external pressure — 26
            II. Exercises in pairs with external pressure — 33
            III. Reaction speed exercises — 35
            IV. Rubber band exercises — 36
            V. Medicine ball exercises — 39
            VI. T-shirt and weight belt exercises — 40
            VII. Metal bar exercises — 41
5. Ball exercises — 43
    I. Basic jumping exercises (no added weight) — 43
    II. Basic jumping exercises (with a weight belt) — 50
    III. Basic jumping exercises (with jelly-rubber) — 51
6. Goal exercises without a ball — 52
    I. General exercises — 52
    II. Specific exercises — 55
7. Goal exercises with a ball — 59
8. Saving shots — 66
    I. Shooting from swimming — 67
    II. Static shooting — 74
9. Saving shots with players' block — 78
    I. Shooting past a block from swimming — 78
    II. Static shooting past a block — 80
10. Goalkeeper in team defence — 84
    I. Combined defence - 6 on 6 — 85
    II. Extra man defence - 6 on 5 — 90
11. Other goalkeeping exercises — 96
12. (Pre)game remarks — 98
13. Statistics — 100
14. Glossary of terms — 105
15. Bibliography — 108

The author is dedicating the book to water polo coaches of all categories. The work presented in the book can be used for all levels of coaching and training of the water polo players.

Main focus was placed on speciality of goal keeping. The exercises were meticulously elaborated, richly illustrated and presented in original way by the author, reflecting his life long experience in water polo.

They have been systematically categorized, knowledgeably chosen and occasionally applied to the work with all the players within the team. Special focus was placed on the defence of the goalkeeper near the block, giving theoretical explanations and suggestions of useful exercises. Additionally, the author has successfully described the role of the goalkeeper in the collective defence throughout the system of combined defence with player less.

Publishing of this work presents a significant contribution to the modest water polo literature collection.

(From review: Prof. Vinko Lozovina, Ph.D.)

1. INTRODUCTION

Goalkeeper in any sport, and particularly in water polo, has one of the most important and most responsible roles in the team. There is truth in the old saying, perpetuated through the water polo circles that a good goalkeeper is worth "half of the team". Coach's technical and tactical ideas are imperatively based on the abilities of the goalkeeper, particularly in zone defence and some aspects of it (eg. partial zone and leaving a "weaker" player to shoot). Instant decisions in which the goalkeeper plays the main role are frequently made during a game. Goalkeeper's successful intervention is a prerequisite for the initiation of individual and team counter attack. In this instance goalkeeper then becomes the first attacker. The speed of his reaction, his tactical maturity and correct passing to a teammate directly affects the efficiency of the attack and indirectly results in a goal being scored. The confidence and support that the goalkeeper offers to his fellow players in such moments is priceless.

The average of goals scored in today's international water polo is between 6 and 8. Most of the important matches almost inherently finish with a minimum difference and goalkeepers timely save in the key moments of the game, when the result "breaks", often gives the advantage and decides the winner.

As the last player in defence, the goalkeeper corrects all mistakes made by the players of his team while the opposition is in attack. Unfortunately the uncorrected mistakes are recorded and remembered as the final score of the game. Goalkeeper is often left alone to do this unforgiving and responsible job himself, particularly in situations where there is objectively no help from his defenders. The success of the entire team largely depends upon his ability, individual characteristics and overall quality of his game.

Professionally organised clubs have noted this a long time ago. Specialised goalkeeping coaches work with goalkeepers while the head coach works with them directly during the team's situational training and practice games. This way the goalkeeper receives special treatment relative to his effect and role in the game.

Elite goalkeepers have, almost as a rule, very "strong" personalities with accentuated psychomotor qualities, strong psyche, heightened perception and notable intellect. They are an authority in their teams, respected by their coaches and fellow players and as such dominantly influence team behaviour and atmosphere before and during a game.

A player with goalkeeping predispositions should work on specific technical and tactical points and complement this knowledge by converting it to the physical form.

According to my statistical indicators average success rate of saves of a good goalkeeper is between 40-50%, quality goalkeeper from 50-60% and elite goalkeeper from 60-70% and very rarely over 70%. This percentage directly affects the reduction of the effectiveness of the opposition's shots on goal. Thus we can statistically show the effect of a goalkeeper to the final result of the game.

The choice of technique and tactical activity of a goalkeeper during the game is strictly guided by his personal characteristics. That is why we say that every goalkeeper has his own style and tactic. In the past there have been two recognisable styles of goalkeeping - the so-called "calm" and "aggressive" styles. The former was distinguished by a group of elite goalkeepers who, apart from their physical abilities, dominated with their thinking abilities, rational and "calmer" movements. Apart from exceptional physical abilities, the goalkeepers with the latter style were noted for their goalkeeping intuition, fullness and "aggressiveness" of their movements. The feature of this style is very hard legwork, high jump and the covering of the entire space between the bars. In such style the goalkeeper's effectiveness depended exclusively on his personal quality and ability to command the entire goalkeeping space without much reliance on the defenders. However, this was also their biggest disadvantage.

Last ten years have seen the development the third style of goalkeeping. This style is totally subordinated to technical-tactical positioning of the goalkeeper in the game. In these coordinated and well-trained schemes of goalkeeping and accurate positioning, goalkeeper is not left to his own devices any more, but is often actively helped by his defenders. Modern aids such as video and computer technology, together with the statistical analysis and calculations of the probability of players shooting to a particular part of the goal, have ensured good grounds in selecting the right goalkeeping style and appropriate tactics. This ensures greater efficiency of the goalkeeper in a "reduced" style of goalkeeping with simplified movements and smaller, shorter jumps. The area of goals to defend lies within the arm span and from side positions the area is even smaller. The defenders block the remaining area of the goal with their arms.

Therefore, the third style of goalkeeping belongs to the newer generation of goalkeepers, adapted to modern water polo and will be discussed in this handbook. The drawback of this type of goalkeeping is in gradual "diminishing" of the goalkeeper, who increasingly depends on the help from his defenders and takes his duties literally limiting the maximal range of saving shots. Problems arise when the attacker shoots in the space blocked by the defender, particularly if he had previously managed to move the defender from the ideal blocking line, and (statistically rare) with surprise, illogical shots from "unreasonable" situations.

Under the current rules of today's water polo, the goalkeeper's role has become increasingly important. Therefore, goalkeeper must not limit himself only to his "narrow" range of actions but must totally adapt and connect to his team's defensive tactics. He must contribute his share in the moments when the help from defenders fails and when he has to show his personal strength and quality.

In this sense the handbook stresses the adaptability to new water polo in terms of technique and tactics but with consideration of the basic premises and rules that must be equal to all goalkeepers and which directly determine their quality. This way the charisma of great water polo goalkeepers will remain alive and with a good chance to be continued.

2. CHOOSING A GOALKEEPER

The criteria and the methods of goalkeeper selection are more strict and complex than those of field players. This is particularly due to the arduous education that follows the selection and which does not allow for improvisation and, even less, for any mistakes. Ideally, goalkeepers are selected among the children of water polo school, at the age between 10 and 12 years and at the end of one or two years elementary swimming school.

Testing and noticing motor abilities on dry land during any basic game or sport (eg. handball, soccer, basketball) precedes the grouping of children in the water polo/ swimming school. On the basis of the talents displayed we can assess children's coordination, mobility, flexibility, reaction speed and their talent for a team game. This would be the first and starting criteria for selecting a goalkeeper.

The potential goalkeeping candidates must satisfy the second set of criteria, based on their current height and the forecast of maximum height at the end of their growth and development. Studies of morphology of water polo players performed so far have shown that their height directly affects their success in the game. It is possible to use a very simple technique to forecast the maximum height at the end of their growth and development within 1% error in accuracy, on the basis of measured height at any time. The formula, unfortunately valid only for boys, is as follows:

$$\text{End (maximum) height} = \frac{\text{Current height x 100}}{\text{Age coefficient *}}$$

Age	1	2	3	4	5	6	7	8	9
Coeff.*	42.2	49.5	53.8	58.0	61.8	65.2	69.0	72.0	75.0

Age	10	11	12	13	14	15	16	17	18
Coeff.*	78.0	81.1	84.2	87.3	91.5	96.1	98.3	99.3	99.8

(If for example we are making selection among boys aged 10 and we wish they reach 190cm as adults, we have to select only those who are at least 148cm tall. To allow greater confidence we can increase the limit by 1 or 2cm.)

Arm reach is another very important factor in goalkeeper selection, linked to the morphological structure of a goalkeeper and his physical constitution.

For determination of the third criteria we move to the pool where we test the children's buoyancy and evaluate the coordination of movements in the water, after which we begin the training of the fundamental swimming techniques: freestyle, backstroke, breaststroke and butterfly. During this process, we must be particularly attentive to the children's ability to implement the breaststroke kicking technique, from which they develop the essence of every technical element of goalkeeping in water polo – the **eggbeater kick** (EBK).

This correct, and I could say innate, movement of legs is created by series of interchangeable single leg kicks in the manner of a breaststroke kick. Its movement begins in the hip joint and is transferred through the ankle joint into the foot and is inherent to all goalkeepers. The kick forms the basis for the goalkeepers "basic position", from which a goalkeeper can easily spring into action, jump above the water, glide across the goal but only if the movements of his legs, arms and trunk are well coordinated.

The last criterion is not related to any objective testing nor it is formed along a set of parameters. This criteria is coach's judgement in how well are the children gifted with a natural goalkeeping intuition, anticipation of situations and whether their goalkeeping movements are coordinated and attuned to the rest of their team (in other words "do they attract the ball or does the ball attract them"). Naturally the overarching priority at a young age is goalkeeper's willingness to become a goalkeeper.

If these criteria are reasonably satisfied and all the necessary conditions for further work set, they are followed by long years of work along the detailed stages in the training program. In this process we follow the development of important psychomotor characteristics such as endurance, strength, speed, flexibility, coordination, accuracy and mobility. Continuous overseeing of the ability of movements and their liveliness in the water helps further development and selection.

Psychometric tests and other forms of measurements of psychological functions are desirable in the later stages of training process in order to establish the level of intelligence, reaction speed, concentration and temperamental characteristics* of selected goalkeepers.

*The most desirable temperament type is sanguine (dexterous, lively, strong, high-spirited, irritable and vehement nature).

3. BASIC THEORETICAL PREMISES AND CALCULATIONS OF OPTIMAL REACH

The correct choice of a place and position of a goalkeeper in goals is an important precondition for successful saves. Theoretically, the goalkeeper should at any moment be positioned symmetrically, that is on the line which halves the angle, formed by the lines connecting the two goal posts and the ball. He then decides to make an appropriate technical intervention to successfully stop the shot.

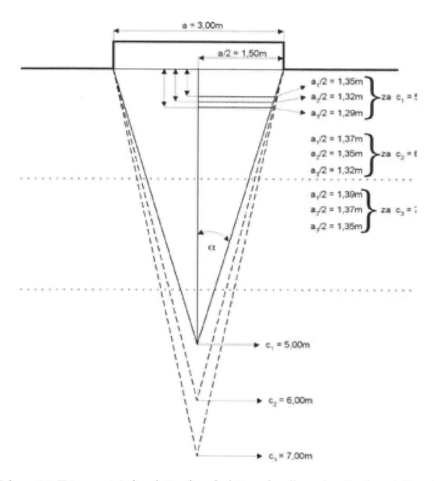

Scheme 3.1: Trigonometric foundation for calculation of goalkeeper's optimal reach (jump)

Distance from the shooter/ Goalkeeper's distance from the goal line (c/b)	Half of the goalkeeper's arm span (1.95m/2) (statistical)	Length of a jump needed for area coverage (calculation) $(a_n/2)$	Length of a vertical jump with a short lateral move (statistical)	Length of a short and fast lateral jump (statistical)	Length of a long and slower lateral jump (statistical)	Reduction of area coverage length by goalkeeper's move from 0.5m to 0.7m (calculation)
5m / 0.5m		1.35m				
5m / 0.6m	0.975m	1.32m	1.15-1.20m	1.35-1.40m	1.55-1.60m	6cm
5m / 0.7m		1.29m				
6m / 0.5m		1.375m				
6m / 0.6m	0.975m	1.35m	1.15-1.20m	1.35-1.40m	1.55-1.60m	5cm
6m / 0.7m		1.325m				
7m / 0.5m		1.393m				
7m / 0.6m	0.975m	1.37m	1.15-1.20m	1.35-1.40m	1.55-1.60m	4cm
7m / 0.7m		1.35m				

The results in the table offer the following conclusions:

1. Total area coverage area between *1.29m* to *1.39m* for a shoot from 5m to 7m is achieved by a short and fast lateral jump of maximum length between *1.35m* and *1.40m* (highlighted column) when the goalkeeper is positioned 0.5m to 0.7m from the goal line.

2. Total area coverage of *1.29m* for a shoot from 5m is achieved by goalkeeper's vertical jump with outstretched arms and a short and fast lateral move, thus reaching the length between *1.15m* and *1.20m* (lightly highlighted cells) if the goalkeeper is positioned 0.7m from the goal line. We assume that because of the ball's diameter of 22cm there is not enough free space for it to pass through.

3. A long, slower lateral jump, from 1.55m to 1.60m is not needed at all.

4. The goalkeeper's move from 0.5m to 0.7m forward from the goal line directly, but not greatly, affects the reduction of the length needed for area coverage (the gain is from 4cm to 6cm; last column). Therefore we can conclude that goalkeeper's greater movement forward is not overly needed. The effect is relatively small while at the same time increasing the susceptibility to a lob shot.

> The following generalisations can be formed from the points above:
>
> ***Goalkeeping style and technique should be based and developed on the short and fast lateral jump.***
>
> The fundamentals of such technique are based on:
>
> a) Maximally hard legwork, allowing a more vertical and relatively high basic position of a goalkeeper.
>
> b) Very little support on arms and hands (hands are slightly submersed)
>
> c) Reaction speed (according to statistical data, a short and fast lateral jump should take between 0.25 and 0.33 of a second, which corresponds to the flight time of a ball, shot from the common shooting distance between 5m and 7m).

The starting point for the above theoretical propositions is the goalkeeper's position in the middle of the goal and where the ball is situated centrally in relation to the goal. In all other cases the goalkeeper will clearly be situated to either left or right side, depending on the position of the ball. Passing of the ball from left

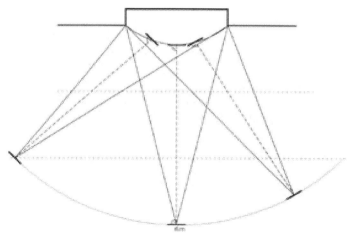

Scheme 3.2: Positioning of a goalkeeper

to right, and vice versa, forces the goalkeeper to slide across the goal into appropriate position along the defined line. Therefore the goalkeeper must always be in a mutually parallel position in relation to the shooter, with simetrala of the angle vertical to goalkeeper's body (see Scheme 3.2).

The goalkeeper is closer to the goal line than when positioned on the sides of the goal than in the middle. To save a shot from extreme side (wing) positions he will sit almost on the actual goal line. Goalkeeper's position must prevent a goal being scored in the "short corner" (corner to the closer post). Such positioning will allow optimal coverage of the diagonal ("cross corner", "cross cage") shot, leaving minimal space for a successful straight shot or a lob. This is the reason for a slight over-coverage of the short corner and smaller distance from the goal line in the Scheme 3.2.

4. PHYSICAL PREPARATION OF A GOALKEEPER

A. INTRODUCTION

Sporting games belong to the category of complex movements, performed most often in cooperation with other team members along with active interference with the players from the opposite team. These movements are complex in terms of both information processing (technical - tactical plans) as well as energy levels (physiological functional characteristics).

Training theory is concerned with these problems and examines certain laws of planning, programming and control of the training process. Players and coaches invest heavily in the process of training to produce the winning results. Training is a group of purposeful and separate exercises, which, over time, produces expected results in a certain period.

The aim of every coach is that the players master all technical – tactical and theoretical knowledge and that they are brought up to the energy levels needed for a successful application in a game.

Success in every sport depends on the morphological structure and build of a player, psychomotor attributes, intellectual, emotional and motivational components, technical and tactical knowledge, theoretical knowledge and a number of other factors. Let us mention only the most important items on the list:

Morphological structure and physical build – play an important role in any sport. As we have already shown, height is one of the factors that directly influences success in a particular sporting activity. Arm reach is another parameter in the morphological structure and very important in goalkeeper selection.

Psychomotor qualities – directly correspond to the ability to perform dynamic movements and their functionality. These qualities enable powerful, quick and lasting functioning of the body systems, all of which have to be well developed in a good goalkeeper. They can be classified as follows:

<u>*Endurance*</u> – relates to the maximum length of an exercise at a particular strength level. Endurance differs among water polo players. Goalkeeper's specific endurance is most clearly demonstrated by the high number of movements on the spot and between the two goalposts and little less in his movements from the goal line to the two-meter line. Endurance is further demonstrated by continuous maintenance and changes of basic body positions, high level of jumping, unbroken concentration and a generally high-energy output throughout the entire game.

<u>*Power*</u> – is the ability of the muscles to produce force during their contraction. By definition it represents the basis for specific endurance, and is the most important psychomotor characteristic of a goalkeeper. Power manifests itself as:

a. Explosive (single movements performed quickly at maximum power),
b. Repetitive (repeating stereotypical movements) and
c. Static (forms of holding in different positions).

a. Explosive power – is a force activating a great amount of energy in a very short time, which is a short activity at great intensity. The coefficient of natural ability to produce explosive power is very high but deteriorates quickly and after the age of thirty even extremely quickly. Explosive power is most important and must be emphasised in goalkeeper training. The chance of greater development increases if we start such training as early as possible. Particular attention must be paid to arms and shoulders but not at the expense of the trunk, which assists in goalkeeper's explosive movements (for example, opening and jump for the ball from the basic position). Of course the attention must also be paid to legs, which also assist in performing explosive movements such as jumps.

b. Repetitive power – underlies the ability to perform as many movements as possible with or without a load. Repetitive power is present in the activities that are longer (in time), but not too long, performed at great intensity at a forced pace. The coefficient of in-born ability to produce repetitive power is very small, therefore increasing the prospect of development. Repetitive power develops relatively quickly through training but drops just as quickly without training. Goalkeeper movements in a "ready position" (discussed in later chapters), based on the water polo goalkeeper's eggbeater kicks, require exceptional repetitive power of legs. Goalkeeper often defends goals in a "ready" position, helped by the eggbeater kick, by stretching of his body, manipulation of his arms and various other repetitive movements.

c. Static power – is the ability to hold a certain load without changing the position of the body or any part of it. Similarly to repetitive power, it also has a very small coefficient of in-born ability to generate it, which means it can improve greatly with training. As a rule, static power is used to stabilise the previously performed movement at the level of repetitive power. For example, fixed stretched position of the body and arms, particularly from the shots coming from extreme wing (side) positions with little shooting angle.

Speed – is another very important element in goalkeeping. It is the ability to perform a move in the shortest time possible or generate a great frequency of movements in a given period. The speed of goalkeeper's movements to and from different positions, movements of separate parts of the body (eg. legs, arms), speed of reaction and starting speed are most important in goalkeeping. The coefficient of the inborn ability is very high. Despite that, practical experiences have shown that it can be developed in junior years. In later years the speed training must be adjusted to the goalkeeper's existing speed and optimal technique.

Agility or flexibility – is important in performing movements with great amplitude. Flexibility and agility subsume the ability to perform such movements as fast as possible.

Coordination – is the ability to harmonise movements in space and time according to the given task, in this case the defence of a goal. There are many different and complex movements in goalkeeping and they require systematic learning and perfection of individual movements.

Alertness – can be defined as goalkeeper's ability to resolve sudden and unexpected situations. A very frequent example is when the ball lands between the goalkeeper and the opposition player. Alertness demonstrates itself in the speed of action, which enables the goalkeeper to win the ball at even odds with the field player.

Accuracy – is demonstrated by the precision of passing the ball to field players or even shooting accuracy at the opposition goal. Timely and accurate pass to attacking players is extremely important and directly affects the team's scoring chances.

B. DRY LAND TRAINING

The effect of a single training session is not measurable, but the cumulative effects of multiple training sessions within a defined time frame are observable and measurable. It is utmost important to tests the initial stage of the athlete's condition (starting condition) in order to design and implement an effective training program. Through training we reach the final stage with a certain degree of probability and the lesser the aberration from the planned result the greater the chance of reaching the final result we have set out to achieve.

Demands of a sporting discipline can be divided into energy demands and information demands. Energy demands predominantly relate to psychomotor abilities of the athlete, while information demands include the sum of technical-tactical abilities of a player-goalkeeper as well as theoretical knowledge.

This chapter discusses several examples of the most basic dry land exercises for improvement of psychomotor abilities of a goalkeeper.

1. Endurance

Endurance is the ability to produce the type and amount of force demanded in the longest possible period. Endurance differs between the field players and goalkeepers due to their different roles in the game, therefore their training is specific and tailored to their basic activities. Endurance is closely related to the overall energy capacity of an athlete, and endurance tests are not very reliable due to its great complexity.

Therefore, before we start with a training program, we must determine the total energy capacity of an athlete in two categories: aerobic and anaerobic. These are two basic sources of energy in a human body. Anaerobic process is the creation and consumption of energy through decomposition of matter without the presence of oxygen. In the aerobic process, the oxygen is present and helps in the decomposition of matter and thus creation of energy.

Anaerobic capacity depends on chemical substances and reactions in the organism and since it is inborn there is relatively little we can do to change it. Aerobic capacity depends directly on the amount of oxygen the body can receive and can be significantly increased with training. Extremely high aerobic capacity is of great value particularly in sports where the action is continuous, over 10 minutes long with high oxygen demand and consumption.

Aerobic capacity is tested and measured in a stable condition with little load, where the inhaled oxygen is sufficient for supply of the working tissues and organs. Testing can be done on a moving track with the assistance of adequate instruments for gradual and progressive increase in the workload.

Testing of anaerobic capacity, also with accompanying instruments, can be done on ergometers with a constant load, by measuring the time of reaching and holding of the maximal intensity.

- Some of the exercises to increase aerobic capacity are different styles of running, with added climbing or jumping tasks. In indoor venues this can be achieved for example by setting various obstacle courses.

Such training sessions are usually conducted at the start of a training period or a season and can be good indicators for planning and programming purposes.

2. Power

Power is demonstrated when a large amount of energy needs to be generated to perform a short, powerful and fast move.

- Exercises and tests that emphasise (and measure) **explosive power** are: long jump on the spot (no run up), triple jump (spot), high jump (spot) and similar exercises.
- Typical exercises and tests for **repetitive power** are: push ups, curls, squats, jumps on (eg. high bench), all of them with or without a load. All of these exercises should be performed at the maximum number of repetitions in a given time or until giving up.
- **Static power** is also very important in the process of training. These exercises are similar to the above mentioned repetitive power sets, using a method of locking and holding of the body in certain positions. They can be performed with or without additional load.

We can divide power on localities such as: power of arms and shoulder region, trunk (abdominal and back muscles) and of legs and hip region. The most important thing is to know how to analyse the structure of goalkeeper's movements and from this observation determine the amount and the type of work needed.

3. Speed

The shorter the time of performing a move within the given amplitude the greater the speed. According to some authors, speed has the coefficient of inborn ability as high as 0.95.

- Typical exercises and tests for speed are various tapping sets with arms or legs and tests of reaction to visual, aural or other signals. We can design exercises for reaction and the speed of performing of tailored to mimic goalkeeper-specific movements (for example, reaction from a squat to continuous shots with tennis balls).

4. Flexibility

Differently to speed, flexibility defines movements of greatest amplitude possible by the condition of the joints.

- Common exercises and tests with which we can develop and measure flexibility are forms of bending, splits, stretching and similar.

5. Coordination

Coordination is the ability to select a reaction most efficient and most suited to the defined goal.

- Stretching, flexibility and alertness exercises enable easier implementation of complex movements as an essential part of goalkeeper's game.

6. Accuracy

By short definition, accuracy is the ability to successfully hit the aimed target. The most important aspect of accuracy for a goalkeeper is the ability of taking good aim, as well as timely noticing and precise passing of the ball to field players, generally over longer distances. This ability is proportionately inverted to the amount of goalkeeper's tiredness and his emotional state.

- Exercises and tests can be relatively easily designed and implemented (for example, precise passing over long (eg. over 12m) distances. These exercises are usually conducted at the very end of a training session.

C. WATER TRAINING

Movement analysis of water polo players has shown the horizontal position is assumed at approximately 35% of the time and the vertical position (water polo eggbeater and other movements performed statically or dynamically in a vertical position) 65% of the time during a game. In case of goalkeepers the vertical component is extremely emphasised while the horizontal component is almost negligible. We can therefore conclude that the types of endurance differ for drivers, centre forwards, centre backs and goalkeepers, as well as they differ in the specific energy requirements during horizontal and/or vertical positions.

From the evidence presented we can establish that endurance is a complex psychomotor faculty. Analysis of the intensity and duration of goalkeeper's work as well as his rhythm during the game shows great amounts of expended energy. According to the conclusions quoted, training of goalkeepers can be divided into two time parts:

- 35% – 40% of time dedicated to general swimming training, adjusted according to each goalkeeper's needs (horizontal stage, development of aerobic capacity and endurance).
- 60% – 65% of time dedicated to specific goalkeeping training (vertical stage, specific anaerobic-aerobic capacity and fitness, endurance and power).

1. General swimming training for goalkeepers – (endurance exercises)

Two swimming styles dominate the swimming training for goalkeepers: breaststroke and butterfly with breaststroke kick. Goalkeepers must master the technique of both styles, particularly the correct kicking technique and the coordination of arms and legs. The technique should not deteriorate at greater swimming speed.

The same rules apply for using the "water polo freestyle" technique (raised head and shoulders), which enables greater control of the space and better handling and guarding of the ball. This particular style is used in exercises over short distances at great speed and high number of turns and starts. Water polo freestyle is also used over longer distances, usually in combination with backstroke during pauses between general and specific goalkeeping exercises as a form of relaxation of legs, which had been under maximal workload.

Coach determines the intensity of swimming training, distance lengths, swimming times and rest intervals as a part of the programming cycle for a particular period.

- Practical experiences have shown that breaststroke distances should vary from 25m – 300m within the 60% – 85% intensity range.
- Usual swim tests for goalkeepers are performed at distances of 15m – 25m (speed) and from 50m – 100m (endurance speed), within the 90% – 100% intensity range.

Picture 4.1: Butterfly, pulling by the hips

Picture 4.2: Eggbeater with vertical kickboard

- Changes of pace and rhythm are often used within swimming sets, as well as gradual increases in physical load (eg. weights). We can use exercises in pairs such as pushing/pulling of hips downward and similar drills to facilitate changes in pace and load. (Picture 4.1).
- These or similar exercises can be used with butterfly or a combination of breaststroke and butterfly styles over the same distances.
- All exercises are often divided into sets of same or similar drills, applying the appropriate rest periods between exercises and sets according to the goalkeeper's heart rate.
- During the rest periods between sets of swimming at distances of 100m or 200m we mostly use legwork exercises: standard breaststroke kick (single or double stroke alternating short/long strokes) and eggbeater kick. The intensity varies with the use of a kickboard, which can also be turned vertically to enable maximal workload for legs. (Picture 4.2).
- Just as we give a greater workload to legs we can use exercises to strengthen arms and shoulders by swimming butterfly (more often than breaststroke) without the use of legs.

2. Specific goalkeeping training - exercises for specific endurance development

Vertical position dominates in these exercises, which can be performed on the spot or with movement, with or without the additional load. **_Water polo eggbeater kick_** forms the basis for all movements in the vertical position. Eggbeater exercises commonly begin in horizontal position by alternating breaststroke kicks with a

Picture 4.3: Basic goalkeeping position

slight bend of pelvis in relation to the trunk. This ensures optimal execution of the kicking action. Arms should be stretched and slightly under water.

Through a transition from a horizontal to an angled position we arrive at the ***basic goalkeeping position***. Head is high above the water, arms still slightly underwater but bent halfway in elbows. Arms are spread at the shoulder width and move in semi circles (scull). Knees are bent and spread apart at the width of the elbows. Legs perform alternate kicks and push from up towards the bottom while feet move in semi circles. (Picture 4.3).

Optimal goalkeeping position is the elevated position (up to the breast nipples in relation to the water level) of the trunk with the upper arm above water at all times to ensure a quick and successful reaction to a shot. By working faster and harder with legs and arms, goalkeeper comes from a low to a "ready", relatively high position above the water level, ready for a fast intervention. From the point of coordination, the basic goalkeeping position is a complex movement, involving legs, trunk and arms.

Picture 4.4: Basic position

The criteria by which we can assess the proper execution of the eggbeater kick are the lack of up-down oscillation of the head and a high and "calm" position in the water. We must pay this detail a great deal of attention as it forms the basis for all starting positions for jumps, glides across the goals and "walking" with arms out performed by goalkeepers.

Picture 4.5: Lateral movement, technique "gliding"

25

Picture 4.6: Walking with "lifts"

I. Exercises without external pressure

- **Goalkeeper's basic position** – Goalkeeper alternately sets in a low, medium and high position, changing the body angle from quasi-horizontal to quasi-vertical position (greater or smaller inclination of the trunk). This type of exercise is commonly performed with forward and lateral movements over distances of approximately 100m – 200m (divided on 25m). (Picture 4.4).

- **Goalkeeper's basic position and lateral movement** – Gliding exercises include short/fast and long/slower lateral movement (glide) to both left and right side. We can practice two techniques: gliding movement (leading hand under the water surface) and skimming movement (leading hand slightly above the water surface). Using a gliding technique, goalkeeper leans with his body in the direction he wants to go to and uses a powerful, simultaneous breaststroke kick, helped by a strong pull with the opposite arm. The leading arm is slightly submerged, extended and pointed as it glides in the desired direction. (Picture 4.5).

Similarly to the gliding technique, the skimming technique starts with the body lean and a powerful kick to the side. This time the leading arm describes an

Picture 4.7: Side jump – right high

approximate semi-circle just above the water surface towards the desired side. This second technique is marginally slower than gliding due to the slightly higher body position but offers a faster hip retraction in order to quickly set in a basic position from which a shot can be saved. It is very important, in both techniques, to retract the hips from a leaning position (lateral movement) to a stable basic position (jumping) as quickly as possible. These exercises are commonly performed over distances of 100m – 200m (divided on 25m).

- *"Walking"* – Goalkeeper walks with his arms outstretched vertically and the water level approximately up to the level of breast nipples. Exercises of

Picture 4.8: Side jump: left low

27

Picture 4.9: Upward straight jump

this type can be performed statically and with movement forward or to the side over distances of 100m – 200m (divided on 15m – 25m) and with occasional "lifts" (body higher out of the water) (Picture 4.6). When performing the exercise correctly, goalkeeper should not display oscillations of body and arms but keep them calm as much as possible and not allow "rocking" from side to side.

- **Jumps** - Jumps can be performed on the spot (statically), for example in series of 9 – 12 repetitions, or dynamically in combination with lateral movement exercises at distances of up to 25m. The main jumping exercises are: side jump (left/right; high and low), upward straight jump, forward straight jump with a hold and lob jump. According to the theoretical propositions outlined in Chapter 3., jumping exercises to either side (left/right) must be based on fast jumps with short leaning of the body to both low and high corners.

  a. *Side jump* – Goalkeeper sets in a "ready" position, produces a single, powerful breaststroke kick to propel his body out of the water and leans with

Picture 4.10: Jump forward ("opening")

his body and the leading arm in the desired direction. He simultaneously pushes off with the opposite arm to add power and length to the jump. He directs his look towards the fingertips of the leading arm as he follows the flight of the ball. Once again, these jumps have to be fast and with short leaning to the side. (Pictures 4.7 and 4.8).

b. *Upward straight jump* – From a "ready" position, goalkeeper propels his body upward with a single, powerful breaststroke kick, outstretches his trunk and extends his arms above his head. This brings his body in a very high position while he leaves his arms half-bent with palms directed towards the ball. (Picture 4.9).

c. *Jump forward "opening"* – Very similar to the upward straight jump, except that goalkeeper outstretches his arms horizontally (possibly towards the sides) and leans his body slightly forward. (picture 4.10).

Picture 4.11: Jump with a hold

29

Pictures 4.12.a and 4.12.b: Lob jump – "opposite" and "close" arm

   d. *Jump with a hold* – Following a jump forward ("opening"), goalkeeper holds a high body position with additional breaststroke kick(s) and possibly a simultaneous slight leaning to one side. (Picture 4.11).

   e. *Lob jump* – As the name suggests, lob jump is used to stop a lob shot. Lob jump can be executed in two ways, depending on the angle of the shooter and the shot itself. Using the "opposite arm" technique, goalkeeper leans backwards from the basic position, sculls with the supporting arm and extends his body together with his opposite arm to stop a falling ball. In this case, he uses his left arm to stop a falling lob shot to his right. (Picture 4.12.a)

   The "close arm" technique is used to stop a rising ball. In this case the goalkeeper rises high vertically and tries to stop the lob shot with his closer arm. In short, he stops a rising lob to his right with his right arm. Both techniques can be used in practice with alternating sides to defend. (Picture 4.12.b)

- **Lateral movement and jump combination** – Goalkeeper makes a lateral move from the basic position, quickly retracts his hips and from there jumps to the side. These exercises are commonly performed over distances of 25m with alternating the sides (left/right) and ways (gliding or skimming) of lateral movements.

- **Walking, short lateral movement and jump combination** – This combination is very similar to the previous exercise. The only exception to the above

Picture 4.13: Jump with pole touch

exercise is that the goalkeeper starts from a walking position (hands above head). On coach's signal, he makes a short lateral move, retracts his hips and jumps from the basic position. Same training notes apply regarding distances and variations of this exercise.

- **Walking and lob jump combination** – From a walking position the goalkeeper sets in the basic position and executes a lob jump to either side with the opposite arm. Same training notes apply regarding distances and variations of this exercise.

- **Jumping with a pole touch** – Coach stands on the edge of the pool with an approximately 2.5m long pole, which he uses to determine the height and direction of the jump. Goalkeeper must jump out quickly and touch the pole with his fingertips. After one jump the goalkeeper resumes the basic position as quickly as possible while the coach sets a new position for a repeat jump

Picture 4.14: Walking with "lifts" and pole touch

Picture 4.15: Arms exercise

as the exercise continues. A wide variety of jumps can be used in this exercise. At first the jumps should be performed on the spot and later proceed to jumps with a preceding glide or other forms of lateral movement. The most common sets consist of approximately 8 – 12 jumps. (Picture 4.13).

- **Walking and lifts with a pole touch** – Similarly to the previous exercise, the goalkeeper must continuously touch the pole with his fingertips from a walking position. As the coach lifts the pole higher, the goalkeeper tries to touch the pole from the same position with outstretched arms and raised body. This exercise can be performed on the spot or with lateral movement in series of up to 20 – 25 seconds. (Picture 4.14).

Picture 4.16: Basic position with pressure on shoulders

Picture 4.17: Jumps with downward hip pressing

- **Arms strengthening exercises** – Goalkeeper puts his feet on the edge of the pool and lies horizontally and face down while sculling hard with his hands. In the middle of the exercise he increases the frequency and strength of sculling, which lifts his upper body slightly above the surface. From this position, and on coach's signal, he extends one arm above the surface, mimicking a jump towards the ball. After a short pause he repeats the exercise by extending the other arm and continues to alternate arms. This exercise is best performed in series of approximately 20 – 25 seconds duration. (Picture 4.15)

II. Exercises in pairs with external pressure

- **Water polo eggbeater with external pressure** – One goalkeeper sits in a basic position while the other goalkeeper stands behind him and pushes his shoulders down. The exercise can be done in multiple series on the spot or with movement on distances of up to 12m, alternating the goalkeepers' positions. (Picture 4.16).

- ***Jumps with hip pressing*** – In this exercise the active goalkeeper sets in

Picture 4.18: Walking with lifts and downward pressing

33

Picture 4.19: Simultaneous arms and legs strengthening exercise

the basic position while the passive goalkeeper stands behind him pressing down his hips. All types of jumps can be practiced here, firstly without a short lateral move (glide) and later in combination with it. These can be performed on the spot or in movement, jumping approximately up to 9 – 12 times after which the goalkeepers change roles. (Picture 4.17).

- **Walking with lifts and downward pressing** – One goalkeeper (active) sets into the vertical position with arms outstretched while the other (passive) goalkeeper pushes his hips lightly downwards from behind. After a few metres of walking, the active goalkeeper lifts his body up to the chest water level (or even higher if the pressing is not too strong). The goalkeepers change roles every 12m. (Picture 4.18).

- **Simultaneous arms and legs strengthening exercise** – Both goalkeepers are active in this exercise. One of them sets in a horizontal position and sculls to keep his upper body above the surface. The other goalkeeper stands in a vertical position with his arms outstretched high (walking), and tries to keep his shoulders as high above the surface as possible. He slowly moves forward, moving his partner with him as well. Goalkeepers change roles every 12m (or every 20 seconds) during multiple sets. (Picture 4.19).

- **Water polo eggbeaters: push, start, and jump** – Both goalkeepers face each other in a horizontal position. They push forward and challenge each other with powerful eggbeater kicks. On coach's signal they split in different directions with a short (4m –5m) burst of butterfly, resume their basic position and make a few fast jumps to both sides. The same exercise can be used with a combination of frog kick and breaststroke swimming. (Picture 4.20).

Picture 4.20: Water polo eggbeater push, start and jumps

III. Reaction speed exercises

- *"Mirror" jumps* – Two goalkeepers stand approximately 3m apart facing each other. One of them leads the exercise by combining and mixing different types of jumps and lateral movements. His partner must react as quickly as possible to repeat the moves of the leader, hence the analogy with a mirror. After a series of 9 to 12 jumps the goalkeepers change roles. When the coach wants to compare the reaction speed of both goalkeepers at the same time he sets them in a position next to each other and observes their reaction to a sound signal. (Picture 4.21).
- *Starts and jumps* – On coach's signal, goalkeeper starts from a "ready" position with a strongly initiated breaststroke kick, swims a few bursting freestyle strokes, stops and resumes the basic position. Immediately after that the coach gives further sound signals for the goalkeeper to jump in the pointed direction. The goalkeeper must do the last jump with a hold (maintaining height above water with additional kick(s)). Goalkeepers can do this exercise without the help of a coach by standing approximately 10m from

Picture 4.21: "Mirror" jumps

each other and, similarly to the previous exercise, have one of them "lead" by showing the direction and the speed of jumps.

IV. Rubber band exercises

Jelly rubber should be round, 10mm in diameter, approximately 10m long and have a loop, which serves as a hold, at each end. The rubber is divided into two

Picture 4.22: Jelly rubber exercises and walking with a medicine ball

Picture 4.23: Jump with jelly rubber

equally long ends. One end is fixed at the edge of the pool while the goalkeeper takes the other end in his hands or straps it around the shoulders and stretches the rubber away from the pool edge as far as possible. Affected by the elastic power of the rubber, the goalkeeper sits in the basic position and begins the exercise(s). All of the following exercises are performed in sets of approximately 15 to 25 seconds with the same pause between them.

a. Jelly rubber around shoulders (hands free)
- *Basic position* – Water polo eggbeater.
- *Horizontal position* – Single and double eggbeater kick (second short and fast kick), a kickboard in an upright position can be used to add greater resistance for extra load.
- *Walking* – Eggbeater and breaststroke kicks (arms outstretched above the surface), a medicine ball can be added for extra load. (Picture 4.22)
- *Jumps* – Left, right, straight up, forward. (Picture 4.23).
- *Combination* – Basic position, lateral move, jump.

b. Jelly rubber in hands (arms loaded while holding in the loops)
- *Basic position* – Water polo eggbeater.
- *Horizontal position* – Single and double breaststroke kick (second short and fast kick).

Picture 4.24: Walking with jelly rubber

Picture 4.25: Jumps with jelly rubber

- *Walking* – Eggbeater and breaststroke kicks (arms outstretched above the surface). (Picture 4.24).
- *Vertical position* – Eggbeater kick, arms spread above the surface and closing them together forwards.
- *Jumps* – Left, right, straight up, forward. (Picture 4.25).

V. Medicine ball exercises

Exercises are performed with a 4 – 5kg medicine ball with the help of a coach standing on the pool deck. The coach assists a goalkeeper by throwing and receiving the medicine ball. All of the series of these exercises are of the same duration as the above jelly rubber exercises.

- **Walking with a medicine ball** – Eggbeater or frog kick, with or without lifts. (Picture 4.26).

Picture 4.26: Walking with medicine ball

- **Vertical position on the spot with arms outstretched above the head** – The coach throws a medicine ball slightly above the goalkeeper's hands, then

Picture 4.27: Medicine ball passing exercises

Picture 4.28: Jump and hold with a medicine ball

slightly to the sides. The goalkeeper must "lift" slightly from the vertical position, catch the ball with two hands and throw it back to the coach. (Picture 4.27).

- **Basic position and jump** – On coach's signal the goalkeeper jumps straight up, receives the medicine ball at the highest point and with extra frog kicks tries to hold the elevation while returning to the vertical position. The coach signals to the goalkeeper to return the ball and repeat the exercise. (Picture 4.28). On coach's signal, goalkeeper jumps high upward from the basic position, catches the ball and immediately returns it to the coach. He has to resume the basic position as soon as possible before a repeat.

- **Vertical position with arms high and jump** – After a certain time (eg. 10s) of maximal vertical position while holding a medicine ball, the goalkeeper returns it to the coach and jumps to pointed directions as quickly as possible after a sound or visual signal.

VI. T-shirt and weight belt exercises

These exercises are commonly performed with a diving weight belt of up to 4kg – 6kg, strapped around the waist, and a thicker, long sleeve shirt to increase the load on goalkeeper's arms. It is important to note that the load must not be too great to affect the basic coordination of movements. All of these exercises, particularly jumps and lateral moves, should be performed along the same principles and remain of similar or equal length as the exercises *without* the additional load. At first, goalkeeper performs these exercises without a ball. After that he removes the weight(s) and begins intense ball training without the extra load.

The main exercises are:

Picture 4.29: Side jump with a weight belt and a shirt

Picture 4.30: "High" butterfly with a weight belt and a shirt

- **Jumps and holds** – Left, right, straight up (elbows half-bent), forward ("opening"), jump with a hold (additional breaststroke kick), lob jump. (Picture 4.29)
- **Walking** – Forward and lateral, arms high/low.
- **Combination** – Lateral movement (glide or skim) and a side jump.
- **Swimming** – "High" butterfly (body high out of the water), up to 25m distance. (Picture 4.30).

VII. Metal bar exercises

In this set of exercises we use metal bars of approximately 10kg to 12kg weight, which can often be found in swimming pools as holders of the false start signal-

Picture 4.31: Walking on the spot

Picture 4.32: Two bar lift

ling flags. Because of the great weight of the bars, goalkeepers mostly do walking exercises with maximal load on legs. The exercises are somewhat shorter (12s to 15s) but still performed in series. The main metal bar exercises are:

- **Walking on the spot** – Arms high (with and without occasional "lifts"), eggbeater or breaststroke kick. (Picture 4.31).
- **Bar lifting (horizontal to vertical)** – On coach's signal, goalkeeper lifts the bar from a horizontal to a vertical position (90°) and holds the position for a few seconds with arms outstretched high above his head.
- **Lateral movement with a bar** – Similar to the previous exercise, except the goalkeeper now holds the bar in a horizontal position slightly above the water and moves his body in short, 45° degrees increments. As he moves he lifts the bar just a little and drops it to the previous level when the move is complete. This corresponds to a short and fast lateral movement he applies to move quickly across the goal.
- **Two-bar lift** – For this exercise we use two bars thus exerting a great load both on goalkeeper's legs and arms. In the starting position, the goalkeeper holds the two ends of the bars while the coach holds the other ends on the pool deck. On coach's signal, the goalkeeper lifts his body up, stretches his arms upward and tries to hold the bars high. After a few seconds he returns the arms to the starting position and repeats the lift in a determined interval. (Picture 4.32).
- **Combination of walking and jumps** – The goalkeeper sets in a vertical position with his arms outstretched above the head and stays in this position for 10s. After that he drops the bar (or gives it to the other goalkeeper) and makes several short and fast side jumps on coach's signal.

5. BALL EXERCISES

Rational movement of the body in order to complete the required motor tasks forms the basis of every (good) goalkeeping technique. A goalkeeper can be effective and good only if his movements are appropriately coordinated. The following exercises are performed out of the goal in order to familiarise the goalkeeper with the correct basic movements. These movements vary depending on the distance from the shooter, the direction of the shot, their speed and power. The exercises are intended as a check of the coordination of the goalkeeping movements and an opportunity to correct any poor technique.

The coach determines and alternates the selection of shots he throws from the edge of the pool towards the goalkeeper. He demands an accurate intervention at every ball until the goalkeeper masters the correct movement. These exercises are repeated in series of approximately 6 to 9 interventions of the same type. Ideally, the goalkeeper should go through the entire range of different types of jumps and other forms of intervention at the ball. At the start, the coach throws the ball without and later with baulking.

There are three basic ways of saving a shot:

a. Catching the ball,

b. "Cushioning" and after catching the ball,

c. Deflecting the ball off the arms, body and head.

During these exercises the goalkeeper must be very focused and set in a slightly elevated basic position. From the basic position he arrives at a moderately angled "ready" position with harder and faster work of his arms and legs. He must keep a calm but tense position during the exercises involving baulking as well.

In the water polo jargon "baulking" is a word to express "lifting of the goalkeeper". By baulking, the coach tries to throw the goalkeeper out of balance (or "disrupt" her basic position) just as it happens in a game situation.

I. Basic jumping exercises (no added weight)

- *Basic position and direct shot at the goalkeeper* – Goalkeeper usually catches the ball with both hands when a shot is directed slowly and directly at him. Both palms should be half-bent with fingers spread wide. Thumbs should be joined, forming a closing angle from the top of the ball.

  Goalkeeper should preferably cushion or deflect hard and fast shots rather than try to catch them. From the basic position the goalkeeper jumps towards the ball with his arms slightly bent and his palms turned towards the ball (expecting the contact with the ball). At the time of the contact he retracts his arms slightly backward to "cushion" the impact of the ball and lets the ball drop on the water in front of him. Such shots can be cushioned with go-

Picture 5.1: Cushioning - dropping the ball down

alkeeper's palm, upper or lower arm. Most importantly, the ball should land in the goalkeeper's immediate vicinity to enable his control over it. The most ideal position to cushion and drop the ball is the downward vertical position. (Picture 5.1).

- ***Basic position and shot to the side*** – When the shot is directed in the high left or right corner of the goal, the goalkeeper reacts at it with a ***short and fast side jump***. The leading arm (travelling towards the ball) is stretched, palm slightly extended and "fortified" by spreading of the fingers. This way the ball deflects off the palm into the corner. It is very important to note that the focus of the goalkeeper is directed solely towards the ball, and not the shooter's arm, by visually following the flight of the ball towards the fingertips. (Picture 5.2).

For low(er) and "bounce" shots the technique differs. To stop these shots the goalkeeper jumps sideways quickly, while extending the arms more towards and *at the ball*, thus closing the angle. This ensures a drop of the ball in the goalkeeper's immediate vicinity and gives him control over it. It is very important that the goalkeeper holds his fingers spread firmly so the ball does

Picture 5.2: Deflecting the ball to a corner

not "drill through" the hand but it rebounds off it in the desired direction. As a rule the goalkeeper should intervene at such shots with one rather than two arms. (Picture 5.3).

- **Basic position and lob shot** – We should distinguish two types of jumps at a lob shot. In the first instance, the goalkeeper catches (or blocks) the ball on its way up (close range lobs). In the second instance, the goalkeeper catches (or blocks) the ball on its way down, most often from lobs further away from the goals.

Picture 5.3: Stopping a bounce shot

Picture 5.4: Close range lob   *Picture 5.5: Long range lob*

For lobs from closer distances, the goalkeeper intervenes with the closer arm by quickly stretching his body upwards and towards the ball. (Picture 5.4).

Due to the longer flight of the ball, lobs from further afield give the goalkeeper relatively more time to intervene. From the basic position he produces a strong breaststroke kick and stretches his body while sculling with the supporting hand. He travels backward towards the diagonal post (real or imaginary) and tries to intercept the falling ball. It is important to note that the goalkeeper should always try to save lob shots from longer distance by extending the opposite arm and a maximal stretch of his body with the leaning/ supporting arms providing the additional (staying) power to the jump. The observations

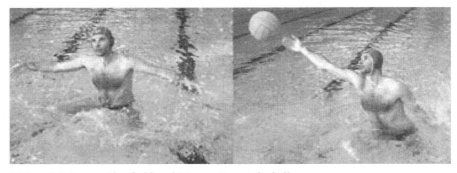

Picture 5.6: Jump with a hold and intervention at the ball

Pictures 5.7a and 5.7b: Lateral glide and shot to the side

have shown that at least 10cm can be gained intervening this way. This is the most complex goalkeeping movement and it takes a lot of practice and good coordination to master it. (Picture 5.5).

- **Basic position and jump with a hold** – On coaches signal the goalkeeper "opens" from the basic position (jumps upwards with his arms outstretched horizontally). With additional (breaststroke) kicks he tries to maintain a high position and intervene at the ball. (Picture 5.6)

- **Basic position, lateral glide and shot to the side** – From the basic position goalkeeper makes a ***fast and short*** lateral move to one side (approximately 1m). He retracts his hips and legs underneath him, sets in a basic position again, ready for a jump. At that moment the coach throws a shot to the side, which the goalkeeper tries to stop. The direction of the move and shot changes with each attempt (left/right). (Pictures 5.7a and 5.7b).

- **Vertical position, glide and jump** – Goalkeeper stands in a high vertical position. On coach's signal he sets in the basic position, glides laterally, quickly repositions in the basic position and from there jumps to the side at the ball thrown by the coach.

Picture 5.8: Stopping a penalty shot

47

Picture 5.9: Semi-vertical position and intervention at the ball

- **Basic position and penalty shot** – Goalkeeper sits in a semi-horizontal, more flat basic position with intense eggbeater kicks. He sculls with hands positioned slightly wider and shallower while his head is marginally retracted backwards. His focus is on the ball. On coach's signal the goalkeeper "opens" (action described earlier) with great force while moving forwards with his body at an approximate angle of 45° (explosive kick, strong body extension and arms wide). (Picture 5.8).

- **Basic position for extra man shots** – Considering the fact that the shots in extra man come from a closer range (2m to 5m average), the goalkeeper sits in a semi-vertical position with maximal leg support from intense and short eggbeater kicks. Again, he marginally retracts his head. His hands are on or just above the surface with elbows bent and palms vertical to the surface, ready for a fast intervention. The coach throws a shot within the goalkeeper's arm reach. Shots should vary from low to high and bounce shots, above head, over and under arms. This goalkeeping technique is used for shots from the outside positions in broad line with the posts as well as the shots from the 2m line. (Picture 5.9).

A different technique is used for shots coming from the side (wing) positions. The goalkeeper sits in a position with body high and arms above his head. In this instance, the coach throws shots directed at the goalkeeper's hands with little deviation on either side.

Picture 5.10: Vertical position and intervention at the ball

- ***Basic position, shots from 2-metre line (backhand, scoop and pull on)*** – Backhand, scoop, pull on shots are usually thrown by centre forwards (2m to 3m distance). Stopping of these shots is a combination of the previous exercise. The goalkeeper has the main two choices of intervention (semi-vertical and vertical with hands above head) to choose from, depending on the situation. (Picture 5.10). The former way of blocking applies when the centre forward has not gained a clear position for a backhand or scoop shot. The latter is used when the goalkeeper is in a clear, direct position to shoot either of these two basic centre forward shots. The same principle applies to pull on shots.

  The coach conducts these exercises with the help of another player, who stands 2m to 3m from the goalkeeper and throws different centre forward/ close distance shots.

- ***Start at the ball (steal)*** – Using a strong, asymmetric breaststroke kick and explosive freestyle stroke(s), goalkeeper intercepts the pass to or gains possession of the ball off the opposing centre forward. The coach throws the ball slightly out of reach of the goalkeeper who has to "steal" and retrieve it as quickly as possible. (Picture 5.11).

Picture 5.11: Start at the ball (steal)

II. Basic jumping exercises (with a weight belt)

After we have assured that the goalkeeper has mastered the basic exercises of jumping with the ball and gained good coordination of his movements, we can proceed with the same types of exercises as described above but with addition of a weight belt. As a rule stated earlier, the weight must not be too great to interfere with the basic coordination of the movements. These exercises can be used in the

Picture 5.12: Jump (with a weight belt) and intervention at the ball

Picture 5.13: Exercises with jelly rubber: jump and intervention at the ball

preparation period when particular attention is paid to power and endurance of legs.

The goalkeeper performs these exercises with the weight belt of no more than 4 – 6kg:

- *Basic position and direct shot at the goalkeeper*
- *Basic position and shot to the side* (Picture 5.12)
- *Basic position and jump with a hold*
- *Basic position and lob shot*
- *Basic position with lateral glide and shot to the side*
- *Basic position and penalty shot*
- *Basic position and shots from extra man positions*

III. Basic jumping exercises (with jelly rubber)

Remarks from the previous section apply in this type of exercise. The goalkeeper puts the rubber around his waist or around his shoulders, fixes the other end to the edge of the pool and sets in a basic position by stretching the rubber to an adequate point of resistance. When using the ball, the coach has to throw it from the water as the goalkeeper is turned towards the edge with his back.

- *Basic position and direct shot at the goalkeeper*
- *Basic position and shot to the side* (Picture 5.13)
- *Basic position and jump with a hold*
- *Basic position and lob shot*
- *Basic position with lateral glide and shot to the side*
- *Basic position and penalty shot*
- *Basic position and shots from extra man positions*

6. GOAL EXERCISES WITHOUT A BALL

The main objective of these exercises is to develop goalkeeper's awareness of space between the posts, the height of the goals and the lines of movement in all directions. They are short in time and length of movements as they take place in the space limited by the two goal posts. The goalkeeper performs these exercises mainly in movement from side to side, just like the game situation would require. We can divide these sets into two categories:

I. General – leg movements, movements in basic position and gliding,
II. Specific – jumps and combinations of glides and jumps.

I. General exercises

- **Movement between posts** – The goalkeeper sits in a ready position and moves with strong kicks and simultaneous, shallow sculling in an arch from the middle position towards one post and back, alternating sides. (Picture 6.1). This type of movement is typical in following short and fast passes of the field players around the perimeter and forms a fundamental element of goalkeeping technique. The goalkeeper repeats the movement several times, moving from one side to the other.
- **Short glides** – These are most commonly used in a zone defence and extra man defence, when the ball is passed from or to the side players and the goalkeeper moves from the middle position to the side position and reverse. As we have already stated in Chapter 4. under "Specific Exercises", lateral movements can be split in two categories: a. gliding (the leading arm remains submerged) and b. skimming (the leading arm forms a semi-circular movement slightly above the water surface). Gliding is applied more commonly than skimming.

Picture 6.1: Middle position

Picture 6.2: Short glide

It is very important to note that lateral **movements must be fast and short** (approximately 1m). The goalkeeper must coordinate his leg movements immediately after a glide/skim. This implies a quick retraction of the hips to allow for a quick intervention/jump at the ball. Short glides are used very frequently and must therefore be paid particular attention to in goalkeeper training. (Picture 6.2).

- *Long glide* – Goalkeeper uses this type of glide when the ball is passed from one side to another in extra man, counter attack, zone defence and any other situation where the flight of the ball is relatively long between the two sides of attack. The long glide technique is identical to the positioning from the middle position to side position described previously. (Picture 6.3). It is important not to be complacent and act slower due to the relatively longer flight of the ball but to perform the movement as quickly as possible. Some goalkeepers use

Picture 6.3: Long glide

Picture 6.4: Walking sideways with "lifts"

two movements with the opposite arm to compensate for greater distance they need to cover. In any case, this is a slow move. I recommend the goalkeeper should make a **short glide/lateral** move, sit in the basic position facing the shooter and "compensate" for the apparent gap in his defence with a short and fast jump to the side (approximately 1.35m).

- **Walking exercises** – These are usually done in the space between the two posts. The goalkeeper holds his hands outstretched, touching the post with both hands at all times. All of these variations can be done with a weight belt (up to 4 – 6 kg):

a. Walking straight with eggbeater kick,
b. Walking straight with frog kick,
c. Walking sideways with eggbeater kick,
d. Walking sideways with eggbeater kick and periodic "lifts". (Picture 6.4).

Picture 6.5: Jump upward

Picture 6.6: Side jump

II. Specific exercises

- **Jumps** – Performed at maximum speed using all basic jump variations and in series of 9 to 12 jumps, with or without a load (eg. weight belt).

a. *Jumps upward straight, left and right* – From the basic position the goalkeeper jumps upright, left, right and returns to the middle position to complete the set. (Pictures 6.5 and 6.6).

b. *Short and fast upright jump (for extra men shots)* – From the basic position the goalkeeper jumps upright and try to protect area within his arm reach. He repeats the exercise several times. (Picture 6.7).

c. *Jumps upward straight (elbow touch)* – From the basic position the goalkeeper jumps upright and tries to touch the bar with his elbow before alternating

Picture 6.7: Short upright jump

Picture 6.8: Jump upward straight and touch of the bar with elbow

the sides. This type of intervention is particularly useful for unexpected shots directed in the area between the shoulders and the side the head, where the goalkeeper is unable to intervene more appropriately with two hands. (Picture 6.8).

d. *Jump with a hold* – After a jump straight up with arms outstretched horizontally; the goalkeeper tries to keep his body high above the water with a second powerful breaststroke kick and leans slightly to one side before resuming the basic position and repeating the exercise. (Picture 6.9).

e. *Lob shot jump* – The goalkeeper sits in the very corner of his goals and from the basic position jumps to the opposite corner (jump with the outstretched opposite arm as in stopping lobs from longer distance). The exercise can be modified by adding initial vertical position (a shot from the wing) before the described jump from the basic position. The goalkeeper continuously alternates corners. (Picture 6.10).

f. *Short glide and jump combination* – The goalkeeper sits in the basic position on one side of the goals. On coach's signal he executes a short lateral glide, re-

Picture 6.9: Jump with a hold

Picture 6.10: Lob shot jump

tracts his hips and sits in the basic position again as quickly as possible. From this position he jumps to the side on coach's second signal. He repeats the exercise from the other side.

Goalkeeper can add to the variety of the exercise by starting in a walking position before performing the above movement (Picture 6.11).

g. *Fast side jumps* – Following the theoretical premises from Chapter 3., goalkeeper's technique should be based on the **fast and short jump** to either side. This exercise is to help the development of this important basic feature.

The goalkeeper sets in the basic position in the middle of the goals and with fast, alternate side jumps tries to touch the two markers (eg. two water polo

Picture 6.11: Walking and jump

Picture 6.12: Fast side jumps and marker touches

caps, tied on the bar approximately 10cm to 15cm from the vertical posts). The markers should therefore be approximately 1.35m to 1.40m from the centre of the goal, which corresponds with the calculation of the length of a fast and short side jump in Table (Chapter 3.). This exercise is very useful and we thoroughly recommended its frequent use (e.g. simulate free throw from 5m in accordance with new Rules). (Picture 6.12).

7. GOAL EXERCISES WITH A BALL

In the previous chapter we worked on exercises that develop goalkeeper's awareness of space and movement between the posts. In this chapter we look at exercises that develop goalkeeper's selection of the appropriate place and the body position in goals as well as the style of intervention. It is well known that the goalkeeper must follow the game action in front of him. He needs to notice the changes in the play and choose the appropriate way of defending his goal in a very short time. Prerequisites for a successful intervention are correct selection of body position and place in goals.

The goalkeeper positions himself in the centre of the goal only when the ball is positioned centrally as well. In all other cases he moves to the appropriate side according to the movement of the ball. The distance from the (potential) shooter determines the choice of body positioning.

The goalkeeper's basic position becomes more horizontal (and lower) as the distance between the shooter and the goalkeeper increases. Inversely, the basic position becomes more vertical (and higher, "ready" position) as the distance between the goalkeeper and the shooter decreases.

We can divide the "shot zone" into two main categories, depending on the distance of the shooter from the goals:

a. Probable shot zone – includes close range (2m to 5m), middle range (5m to 7m) and long range shots (7m to 9m),

b. Shots outside the realistic shot zone (over 9m).

Picture 7.1: Intervention at the shot from the middle position

Pictures 7.2a and 7.2b: First and second type of blocking a scoop

For this type of exercises the coach is the water, surrounded by several balls at a certain distance from the goalkeeper. As he shoots series of shots at the goals he seeks from the goalkeeper to intervene at each shot by a technically correct placement and body position in goals. The coach varies the distance and selection of shots in series. Of course, a field player (or another goalkeeper) can substitute the coach as the shooter while the coach observes the exercise from the pool deck.

- ***Close range shots (2m to 5m)*** – Shots from close range (from the middle and both sides) are the hardest to stop due to the closeness of the shooter and high-ball speed.

Picture 7.3: Stopping a penalty shot

a. *Shots from the middle position* – Goalkeeper sits high in the "ready", semi-vertical position in the middle of the goals and marginally in front of the goal line. His arms are on or slightly above the water surface, palms turned vertically and ready for a quick block. As the player shoots the goalkeeper "opens" with his body upward with a fast and powerful breaststroke kick. At the same time he extends his body and tries to meet the ball with his arm(s) outstretched. Close range shots from middle positions are usually deflected rather than caught or "cushioned". Apart from simple straight shots, the coach can combine other likely shots from this range such as backhand, scoop, roll out and pull on shots. (Picture 7.1).

b. *Scoop and backhand shoots* – When blocking scoops and backhands, goalkeeper decides whether to intervene in a semi-vertical position (first type – Picture 7.2a) or in vertical position with arms above his head (second type – Picture 7.2b) according to the situation. The first type is commonly applied when the attacking centre forward has not set in a particular position for either a scoop or a backhand shot. The goalkeeper uses the second type when the attacking centre forward is in a clear position to execute either of these shots by positioning himself in the predictable path of the ball.

c. *Penalty shot* – Goalkeeper sits in a semi-horizontal, more flat basic position with intense eggbeater kicks. His hands are positioned slightly wider and scull very shallow, while his head is marginally retracted backwards. His focus is on the ball. On coach's signal, the goalkeeper "opens" (action described earlier) with great force while moving forwards with his body at an approximate angle of 45° (explosive kick, strong body extension and arms wide). (Picture 7.3). As an indication the goalkeeper should lean slightly to his right if the shooter is a right-

Pictures 7.4a and 7.4b: Straight and lob shot from the side at close range (2 to 5m)

hander and left if the shooter is a left-hander. If the goalkeeper anticipates a bounce shot, he jumps low and wide forward to close the shot by shortening the bounce angle, vice versa, if he anticipates a high shot, he jumps high (frequently for penalty shot from 5m).

d. *Shots from the side* – These can be straight as well as lob shots. Goalkeeper stops them by positioning his body to close the post in the nearer corner, commonly known as the "short corner". (Picture 7.4a). As the angle (small) and the distance (close) of the shooter allows, he sits in a vertical position with his hands above the head, ready to block a straight shot. He stops any diagonal or cross-goal shots with a fast extension of his arm in the desired direction in order to cut the angle of the shot. (Picture 7.4b).

e. *Lateral movement from the side* – To do this exercise correctly the coach needs additional two shooters, three in total. The goalkeeper positions himself in the short corner with hands breaching the surface, ready for an intervention. The first shooter, from the side position, tries to commit the goalkeeper with a con-

Picture 7.5: Middle position, middle (long) range shot

Picture 7.6: Lob shot from the side

vincing baulk and pass the ball to either the player in level with the closer post or to the player in level with the farther post who shoots immediately. The goalkeeper follows the flight of the ball with a lateral glide or skim, adjusts his body position and tries to save the shot.

- **Middle (5m to 7m) and long (7m to 9m) range shots** – Middle and particularly long distance shots are the most common types of shots in water polo, and as such deserve particular attention in training. They come from the probable shot zone and mostly during a 6 on 6 attack. Middle range shots (5m to 7m away from the goal line) are somewhat less numerous. They most often come after a drive, screen or a pick by the attacking team as well as set extra man situations.

  Goalkeeper generally deals with both types of shots in the same way. The only difference is the inclination of his body and the support on his arms. As the distance of the shooter from the goal increases so does the goalkeepers support on arms and his basic position becomes slightly more horizontal with his hands slightly wider. However, even the long range shots can be very fast and powerful and a greater than needed reliance on arms could reduce their speed and prevent a timely intervention. These shots are generally shot from the middle of the perimeter and rarely from the (extreme) side positions.

  a. *Shots from the middle* – Goalkeeper sets in the basic position slightly ahead of the goal line (0.5m to 0.7m) towards the shooter. This way he optimally cuts the shooting angles while preventing a vulnerable exposure to lob shots. The coach (or the assisting player/ goalkeeper) firstly shoots without and later with baulks. (Picture 7.5).

  It is most important to note that the goalkeeper should strive to remain "calm", that is not to lose the balance in his basic position due to the baulking, at the

63

Picture 7.7: Shots from outside extra man positions

cost of perhaps a small delay in intervention if the ball is shot immediately, with no baulks. An experienced goalkeeper can sense such quick, "off the hand" shots with no baulks, which are more rare than shots with some form of baulking.

b. *Shots from the sides* – Shooter sits on a set distance approximately 1.5m outside the line of either the left or right post. Goalkeeper sits on the basic position according to the shooter and slightly towards him. His position must not allow conceding a goal in the short corner. At the same time, this position optimally prevents a clear shot to the opposite, diagonal corner and or a lob shot. Considering the shooting distance is relatively big, the goalkeeper should attempt to stop any lob shots to the far corner with the opposite arm (arm closer to the nearest post), kicking back to stop the falling ball. Please note the remarks on the lob shot defence in Chapters 4. and 5. (Picture 7.6).

c. *Shots from outside extra man positions (5 and 6 in 4:2 attacks)* – Player shoots from the area within the line of posts approximately 5m away from the goal line. Goalkeeper sits in a semi-vertical position with his hands on or slightly underneath the surface. Shots are directed interchangeably and in different directions (high, low, above the head, under the arms, over the shoulders, bounce shots) into the area of goalkeeper's arm reach. (Picture 7.7).

d. *Lateral movement from the side* – Goalkeeper sets in the short corner in a semi-vertical position. The first shooter stands on approximately 5m to 6m outside of goals and tries to commit the goalkeeper from the side (wing) position to the short corner. As he passes the ball to his partner in diametral position on the opposite side, the goalkeeper executes a short lateral glide, quickly retracts his hips and jumps with the outstretched arm from the basic position. The shooters can change their positions and the direction of the pass after several attempts.

e. *Shots from extreme (deep wing) side positions* – Due to the greatly unfavorable position of the shooter (extremely low shot angle) shots from these positions are quite rare. Lobs are a more common shot choice rather than straight shots. To save them easily, goalkeeper sits in the basic position with his hands underneath the surface. This allows an easy intervention at a straight shot as well as a lob shot and a possible lateral movement across the goals should the shooter pass the ball off.

■ ***Shots outside the probable shot zone (over 9 meters)*** – Coach should use a player with a hard and fast shot to assist with exercises for this type of shots. Shots from over 9m away from the goal line are usually intended as a surprise or at the expiry of the time for attack (30s shot clock or quarter time). Goalkeeper sits a semi-horizontal position, slightly more forward from the goal line than it is the case with long and middle range shots. His head is lifted well above the water while allowing a slightly greater support on his arms, warranted by the relatively longer travel of the ball, hence the extended time for intervention. Shots from great distances should preferably be caught or cushioned and not deflected in the corner, unless of course the quality of the shot requires the goalkeeper to do so.

8. SAVING SHOTS

So far we have discussed the theoretical and practical side of goalkeeping technique. In this chapter we will try to discuss several conclusions from previous chapters and apply them directly to the goalkeeper facing the shooters. Mastering of goalkeeping technique is a lengthy and demanding task but the goalkeeper can be effective and thus expect a good result only when his movements are finely tuned. The examples of shooting exercises offer an excellent opportunity to assess the quality and correctness of goalkeeper's work. There should be no room for poor improvisation and mistakes in training methods.

Before we start looking at the specific exercises we need to make some general distinctions between several categories of shots according to their type and position in relation to the goal. Firstly, a shot is the end result of an organised attack in order to score a goal. It can be shot from a static position, from movement or an immediate shot following a stop in/ of the movement. The most common shots in water polo are static shots, which come from players in the probable shot zone. They can be directed at the goals from the central, side and wing position, using a variety of ball speeds and trajectories (straight-fast shot, lob, semi-lob etc.) and aimed at different parts of the goal (low, high, above head etc.).

Wrist shots are mainly shot from close range (2m to 3m from the goal line). They can be very quick and effective albeit often inaccurate (backhand, scoop, pull on).

Elbow shots are characterised by the fast action of both upper arm and forearm and most commonly used from close to middle range (3m to 5m). The most important feature of these shots is their speed by which they surprise the goalkeeper.

Shoulder shots are executed by the entire arm (stretched or bent in the elbow), including the shoulder joint, and are the hardest (in terms of force and ball velocity) shots, most often shot from distances of 6m and above. The shooter gains additional control of the ball by gently squeezing it with his fingertips, while the movement of his palm determines the direction of the shot and further accelerates the ball.

Slow fasts, or "delay" shots, are a modified version of shoulder shots. The arm movement is initially marginally slower but in the ball releasing stage quickly accelerates and, with the help of a quick wrist action, thus surprises the goalkeeper.

The trajectory of lob shots is parabolic. Lob shots are most commonly shot to capitalise on goalkeeper's bad positioning in goals. There are two major groups: close range lobs with a short and fast ball flight (goalkeeper tries to intercept a rising ball) and long range lobs with a long and slow ball flight (goalkeeper tries to stop a falling ball).

The most common shots from the movement are push shots (ball picked up either from the top or bottom) and bat shots, usually shot from close range (2m to 3m).

Shooting

For the purpose of the following exercises the coach can split the players (shooters) into groups and coordinate their activity as the exercise progresses. As well as demanding from the goalkeeper quick and intensive reactions, the coach should demand and engage the players in a very good quality work out.

Exercises are fragments of game situations, practised many times over. This is mutually beneficial to the goalkeeper and the player. The goalkeeper gets to practice saving all types of shots from different positions while the players, adapted to a particular spot they shoot from, develop their shooting technique and through increased effectiveness improve their confidence. These are some of the prerequisites for a successful game performance.

I. Shooting from swimming

1. Players form three groups with equal number of players and balls in each group. They position themselves on the left, middle and right side of the field at approximately 10 meters away from the goal (Scheme 8.1). On coach's signal a player from the group on the right shoots, collects the rebounded ball after the shot and goes at the back of the queue. After a certain time or number of repetitions the groups rotate their positions to allow every player to have equal number of shots from each of the three positions. Types of shots vary and below are some suggestions on their variety:

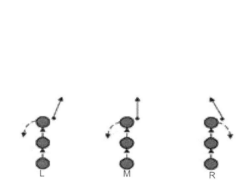

Scheme 8.1: "3 groups – 3 positions" shooting

a. In the first series of shots, players swim to 2m – 3m line and choose an "off the water" (ball only slightly and quickly lifted onto the hand for a shot) shot of their own. In the second series, the players shoot a scoop shot (right handers) from the left, bat shot or push shot from the middle and roll out (backward or to the side) shot from the right side position.

b. Players swim to 4m – 5m line, quickly stop and shoot a quick elbow shot (see above for its description). From the side positions, players alternate between shoots to short corner, cross-goal (diagonal) or lob shots in separate series.

67

From the middle position, players alternate between low and/or bounce shots in the first, high shots in the second and a combination of all shots, including lobs, in the third series.

c. Players swim, stop and immediately direct a powerful shot from 6m – 7m. Similar to the previous set, players alternate between shots to short corner, cross goal (diagonal) or lob shots in separate series while from the middle position players alternate between low, high and lob shots. In the second instance player's baulk before every shot, while in the third variety they use all of the above combinations of shots. The alternation between off the hand (immediate, no baulk) shots and shots with baulking creates a game like situation where the goalkeeper does not know what shot to expect.

d. Balls get divided equally between the middle (M) and right (R) groups. A player from R and L (left) groups start swimming simultaneously, R with the ball. They both stop on 6m – 7m, R tries to commit the goalkeeper with baulks and passes across to L who immediately shoots. M swims to the 6–7m line, stops and either shoots immediately or tries to baulk to throw the goalkeeper off balance before the shot. After several series the players rotate positions to allow all players even exposure to all shooting positions and the goalkeeper to practice saving shots from different directions and players.

2. Players line up in one group in the middle (M). The first player swims to 2m line, diverts sharply to the left, jumps up high and receives the ball from a passer (still in group M) for a tap in. The second player springs to the right and receives a high pass for a pull on shot. In both cases the goalkeeper knows where the shot is coming from and tries to save the ball by correctly closing the shooting angle (moving up and closer) with his body high above the surface and arms ready for intervention. (Scheme 8.2).

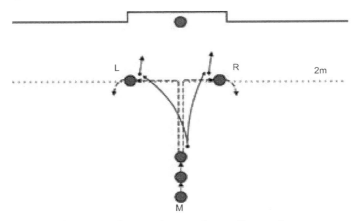

Scheme 8.2: Shooting from 2m line, pull on and jump

3. One player stands on 2m on the left (L), in line with the post, and one player on the right (R) side of goals. The remaining players line up in the middle (M), approximately 10m away from the goal, with the balls. A player from M passes the ball to R, swims several strokes towards the goal, and receives the ball from R and shoots. After the shot he rotates the player at the R position to pass the ball to another player. The next player from M does exactly the same except he passes to and receives the ball from L position, to which he goes after the shot to pass to another player. Goalkeeper must at all times be set to the position of the ball and therefore move from the middle position to the sides and back in every instance. Shots can either be immediate, off the hand in the first series and with baulks in the second series. (Scheme 8.3).

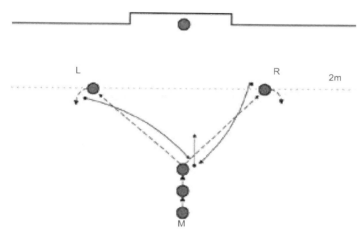

Scheme 8.3: Passing – shooting from M and side (L, R) positions

a. This exercise is almost identical to the previous one. The only difference is that now the player from M swims a few strokes, stops and tries to commit the goalkeeper with baulks before passing the ball to the player at R, who shoots from the side position. Exactly the same goes for the shots from L. As they pass, players from M swim towards the side the shot comes from and replace the shooter, who returns back to the middle group (W) after the shot. By making short lateral moves the goalkeeper practices defence of the short (near) corner, which should be his priority over cross-goal shots.

4. If we are dealing with a larger group of players, we can divide them into two groups to perform the above (3.a) exercise more efficiently. One group practices exclusively shots from the left and the other from the right side. Groups alternate their shots and positions after a set period of time or a number of repetitions to allow for equal shooting opportunities. (Scheme 8.4).

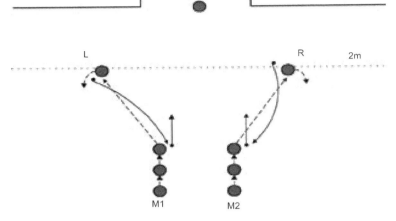

Scheme 8.4: Passing – shooting in two groups from M and side (L, R) positions

5. All players, except two players who stand on the 2m line in L and R positions, line up in group M on approximately 10m. A player from group M swims a few strokes towards the goal, baulks the goalkeeper and passes the ball to the player at R. The player at R commits the goalkeeper and passes the ball to L, who shoots immediately. After the shot the players rotate counterclockwise by one position while the shooter goes to the back of group M and waits for his next turn. Of course, the direction of the pass can be changed in the later series of repetitions. The goalkeeper must at all time follow the ball with his body movement and move laterally according to the position from where the shot is likely to come. (Scheme 8.5).

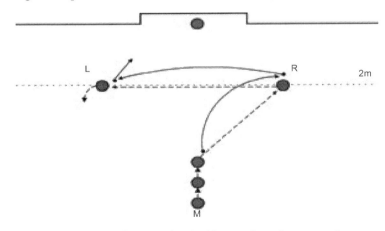

Scheme 8.5: Shooting after double pass (lateral movement)

6. All players, except two players who stand on the 2m line in L and R positions, line up in-group M on approximately 8m. On coach's signal the player from M swims towards position R, while R swims along the 2m line to the position M1 in the middle of goals. Immediately as they set in their (new) positions, a pass comes from 8m (group M) to R, who passes immediately to M1 for a quick shot. The shooter retires to the end of group M. The next player from group M does almost exactly the same, except that he goes to position L instead of R and the player from L swims along the 2m line to M1 for a pull-on shot (if right handed). (Scheme 8.6).

This is a very useful exercise as it contains elements of specific combinations in extra man play. The goalkeeper must follow the ball at all times and adjust his position according to its position and the position of the passer/shooter.

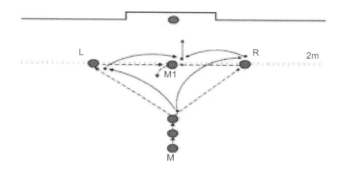

Scheme 8.6: Shooting from the middle after double pass (lateral movement)

7. One player sets in side position approximately 10m away from goal, outside the line of the right post (position P; "passer"). Remaining players line up in the group M on 10m as well. A player from M swims several short strokes towards the goal, makes a 90° turn (hook out) and after several strokes in the new direction turns on his side (or back) in order to receive the ball from P. As he gets the ball he directs a straight, off the hand shot at the goal and retires to the end of group M until his next turn. After several rounds the players can change the passer at P. In subsequent series the direction of the pass can be changed, i.e. passes come from the left and shooters hook out to the right before a shot. A chaser/defender can also be included in the exercise, following the shooter at approximately 1m distance. (Scheme 8.7).

This exercise contains elements of a counter attack (fast break). The goalkeeper must follow the ball at all times and adjust his position according to its position and the position of the passer/shooter.

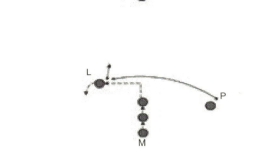

Scheme 8.7: Shooting after a pass from the right

8. The first player sets in the M1 position (2m line, middle of goals) and the second player in the M2 position (6m – 7m line, middle of goals). On coach's signal the second player takes off in a variety of directions (very short distance moves) of his choice, stops, receives the ball from M1 and shoots. After a series of approximately 10 shots he replaces the player at M1 to pass the ball. A chaser/defender can be included in the exercise, keeping approximately 1m distance from the shooter. In another variation of this exercise the balls can be passed to the centre-forward position (M1), which tries a variety of shots. (Scheme 8.8).

This exercise is most useful when the coach wants to maximise the shooting/passing load of a limited number of players while exposing the goalkeeper to a variety of continuous fast shots. The goalkeeper must try to react to and stop as many shots as possible.

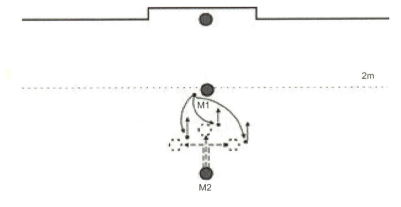

Scheme 8.8: Shooting from the middle after a pass from M1 (centre-forward)

9. One player sets in position M, approximately 8m from the goal. Two pairs of players on each side (L1-L2 and R1-R2) set on a distance of approximately 6m from goal, just outside the line of the goal posts. Player at M baulks the goalkeeper while L1 and L2 execute a move equivalent to a "screen". As they set, M passes the ball and L1 shoots. The same applies to R1 and R2 (R1 is preferably a left hander), who shoot immediately after. During the exercise the players are free to move into different positions. At first, this exercise is done without defenders in order to master the timing of the screen and the pass but once the players are competent defenders can be included. (Scheme 8.9).

This exercise is useful in adjusting the goalkeeper and the players to examples of screens and shots from these positions. The goalkeeper must follow the ball at all times and adjust his position according to its position and the position of the passer/ shooter.

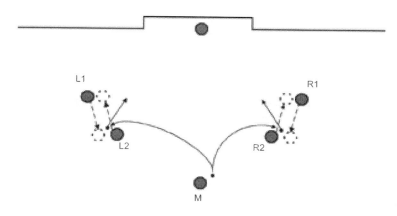

Scheme 8.9: Shooting from the side after a screen

10. Four players position themselves on the perimeter (within the probable shot zone) with only one ball in the pool at the time. They make short moves in any direction, receive an accurate pass from their fellow player and shoot. The shooter contests the rebound, gathers the ball and immediately passes to another player who is ready to shoot. The players and the goalkeeper keep a high intensity throughout the exercises. After a certain time interval the coach rests or changes the group or individual players.

The exercise is a synthesis of the ones outlined in this chapter. If done correctly and under adequate supervision and guidance by the coach who stands behind the goals with spare balls, this exercise can be very effective for both players and the goalkeepers. (Scheme 8.10).

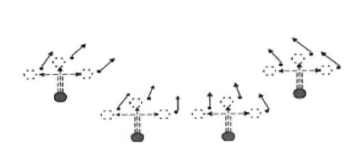

Scheme 8.10: Shooting with swimming and rebounds

II. Static (positional) shooting

1. The players form a semi-circle within the probable shot zone. Each player has a ball, which he throws, usually without baulking, at the goals on coach's signal. The emphasis of the exercise is on the speed of goalkeeper's reaction. The exercise can be modified to include baulking, changing shooters as well as the order and direction of shooters. (Scheme 8.11).

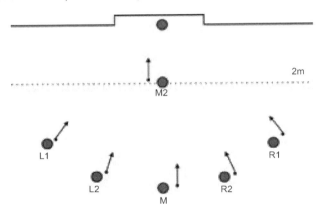

Scheme 8.11: Static shooting within the probable shot zone perimeter

Examples of variations:

a. On coach's signal, the shooter on the far left starts, player next to him continues until the far right shooter has his shot. Shooting can be done with or without baulking.

b. Coach stands behind the goal and points out the player who shoots immediately. This exercise requires the goalkeeper to be very alert to notice and react to shots as he does not know who the next shooter is while the coach is standing behind his back.

c. Cross over shooting in pairs, for example, R2 - L1 (and reverse); L2 - R1 (and reverse) and any other combinations that require the goalkeeper to quickly move across the goals to adjust for and save the next shot.

2. This exercise is identical to the previous one, with the addition of a centre-forward (CF). CF can have typical CF shots (eg. scoop, backhand) as well as he can pass the ball to the players on the perimeter. (Scheme 8.12).

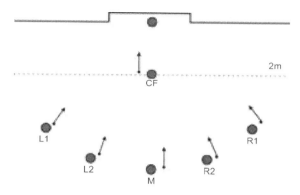

Scheme 8.12: Shooting from the perimeter combined with CF

The coach can vary the shooting combinations to provide a purposeful, game like exercise.

3. Wing players and drivers take their extra man attacking positions. They exchange passes, on their side of the field, and alternate shots at goals. (Scheme 8.13).

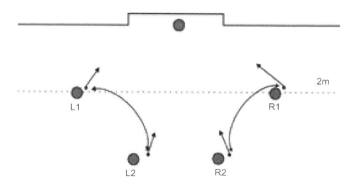

Scheme 8.13: Shooting from extra man positions (same side)

4. For the following set of exercises we need six players in their respective extra man attack positions. The aim of this set of exercises is to practice goalkeeper's movement as well as players' passing and shooting in extra man situations. (Scheme 8.14).

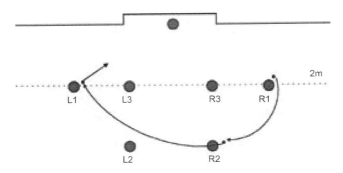

Scheme 8.14: Shooting from extra man set up (4-2)

a. The coach divides the players in two triangular groups (L1, L2, L3 and R1, R2, R3). L2 starts off with a baulk, passes to L1, who passes to L3 for a pull on shot from the post. Players on the right perform the same combination on their side (R2 to R1 to R3). Groups shoot in turns.

b. R1 has five balls and passes them to players in other positions in order. The players shoot immediately after they receive the ball from R1.

c. R1 has five balls and passes them for a double pass. For example, the pass may go from R1 to R2 to L1. The objective of each player is to commit the goalkeeper with a convincing baulk before passing the ball off so the goalkeeper moves around the goal following the ball.

5. Extra man play is very important if not dominant in today's water polo. The success in this aspect of the game greatly affects its final outcome. In order to train the goalkeeper as much as possible in successful extra man defence, particularly in saving shots from the outside positions (5 and 6), we can use the "short goal" exercises. We can tie a rope (rubber, ribbon, tape or any other similar aid), weighted by a small weight to ensure a straight line, approximately 30cm to 35cm (one foot) inside the goal on the horizontal bar. The goalkeeper sits approximately 50cm – 60cm ahead of the goal line and saves the area within the reach of his arms. As a rule, he sits is a semi-vertical position with his hands almost on the surface, ready for a quick intervention. Jumping out of this position is very short and fast. The players, split into two groups and standing 5m away from the goal in line with the two vertical posts, alternately direct their shots into the area of goalkeeper's reach (the two parts near the posts would ideally be covered by defenders' arms).

After their shot the players return at the back of the row and groups rotate after a certain number of shots or a time interval. (Scheme 8.15).

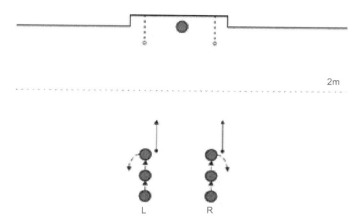

Scheme 8.15: "Short goal" shooting from the outside (L and R) positions in extra man attack

6. Three players set in regular attacking positions on the perimeter (R, M and L), approximately 6m – 7m away from goals. They pass the ball between them, varying direction and speed of their passes, try to commit the goalkeeper with good baulking and shoot at the best opportunity for scoring a goal. The goalkeeper must practice short and fast glides, quick re-positioning and adequate jumping intervention. This type of play is most common in a zone defence. (Scheme 8.16).

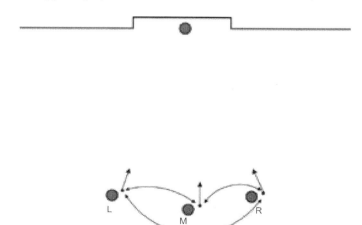

Scheme 8.16: Shooting from the perimeter with passes between R, M and L (zone defence)

9. SAVING SHOTS WITH PLAYERS' BLOCK

Chapter 8. covered some basic moving and static shooting exercises without the participation of defenders. There are two basic defending system in water polo: *pressing*, or "man on man" defence and *zone* defence. The main objective of pressing is not to allow the opposition players to freely organise their attack and to prevent shots at goal. The main objective of zone defence is to cover the area between the ball and the goal by appropriate positioning and blocking of shots with one or two arms.

Blocking is an important element of water polo game. When blocking with a single arm, a player sits in a vertical position with one arm raised and slightly bent in his elbow, ready to block the ball and/or the space. He sculls hard with his opposite arm to support the high vertical stance. When blocking with two arms, a player sits in a vertical position with both arms raised above the surface and slightly bent in elbows. However, the arms must not be in a position where it would be easy for the ball to touch both arms at the same moment and potentially cause a penalty shot.

In the following exercises we will mostly use the **one arm block** as the ideal reaction of the defending player against a shot. As a matter of convention players **defend space**, which means they may block with **left or right arm**, depending on the situation at hand and without forcing a block with the **"mirror image"** blocking at all times.

I. Shooting past a block from swimming

1. Players split into two groups (R and L) at approximately 10m away from the goal and with 3m between them, in line with the vertical posts. Two defenders stand on approximately 5m metres and attempt to block the shots by the attackers. The L player lifts his right or left arm (**"mirror image"**) and R lifts his left arm (**"mirror image"**). The goalkeeper is in a semi-vertical position and ready for a quick jump and/or short and fast glide across the goal. Examples (Scheme 9.1):

a. Both players simultaneously swim toward the goal and shoot one after another, in a short interval, with or without baulking. After their shot, the players return to the back of the line up.

b. The two groups split further apart. After a short swim, player on one side baulks the goalkeeper and passes to the player on the other side for a shot. Groups alternate shots and positions.

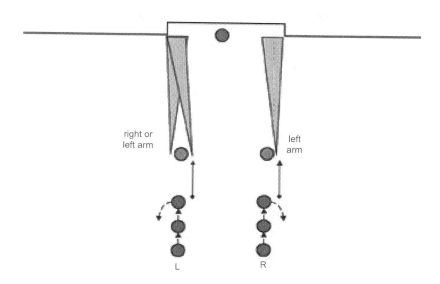

Scheme 9.1: Shooting past a block in two groups with and without a cross-pass

2. A similar exercise to the above, with the addition of the third, middle group. The R, M and L groups are separated by 3m. Three defenders block the shots according to the agreed scheme (e.g. the middle defender blocks goalkeeper's left corner with his left arm – **"mirror image"**) so the goalkeeper can anticipate the direction of the shot (in the middle or in the right side). After several attempts, groups can alternate positions and defenders. (Scheme 9.2).

Examples:
a. All three players (R, M and L) swim towards the goal, stop and shoot in order with or without baulking.
b. All balls are thrown on the right side of the attack. The R player swims in, passes to M, who passes further on to L for a shot. The aim of this exercise is to achieve fast movement of the goalkeeper towards his right. However, by defenders blocking the corners, the goalkeeper's movement becomes shorter and therefore faster. This exercise can be repeated from the other side or any other combination of passes.

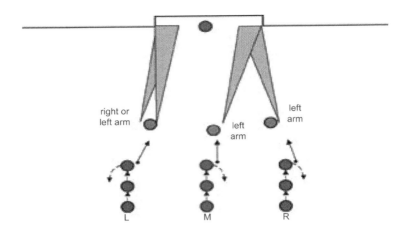

Scheme 9.2: Shooting past a block in three groups with and without a cross-pass

II. Static shooting past a block

1. Four players set in R1, R2, L2 and L1 extra man positions with a ball each. Two defenders sit on 2m in line with the two posts and attempt to block the shots. The goalkeeper sits in a semi-vertical position with hands only slightly below the surface and ready for a quick intervention within his arm reach and short, fast slides across the goal.

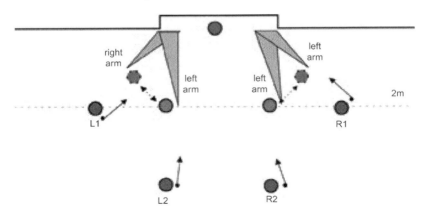

Scheme 9.3: Shooting past a block in extra man attacking set up (4 on 2)

Examples (Scheme 9.3):
   a. R2 baulks the goalkeeper, passes to R1 who takes a shot. The defender in front of them sits in a vertical position with a raised left arm and adjusts his

position according to the shooter by sliding along the shortest possible line to and from the 2m line. And vice versa, when the ball is at R2 he extends also his left arm – **"mirror image"**, standing on approximately 2m line. Players on the left (L1 and L2) repeat the exercise on their side while the defender in front of them blocks the space with his right arm (shot from L1) and with his left arm – **"mirror image"** (shot from L2). At all times the goalkeeper follows the ball and stops all shots directed in the area of his responsibility.

b. A similar exercise to the above, only this time the pass is longer as it goes from, for example, R2 after a baulk or two, to L1 for a shot. The defender on goalkeeper's right blocks the right corner of goal at times. When the ball is at R2 he extends his left arm, standing on approximately 2m, while he blocks a shot from L1 from inside 2m with his right arm. The exercise can be repeated on the other side with the defender on goalkeeper's left blocking the left side of the goal with right (shot from L2) and left arm (shot from R1) respectively.

2. A group of three players set in their perimeter positions (R, M, L) in a regular attack (6 on 6). Three defenders block their shots at an agreed distance. The defender on goalkeeper's right (A) blocks goalkeeper's right with his right or left hand (**"mirror image"**) while the defender on the other side (C) blocks with his left arm. The middle defender (B) blocks with his left arm most frequently (with the **"mirror image"**, eg. right handed shooter blocked with defender's left hand and vice versa). (Scheme 9.4).

Attackers are free to baulk and commit the defenders and the goalkeeper, and shoot when they feel they have the best chance of scoring a goal. The goalkeeper follows the ball at all times with **short, fast glides** across goals and stays in a semi-vertical position, ready for a quick intervention, at all times.

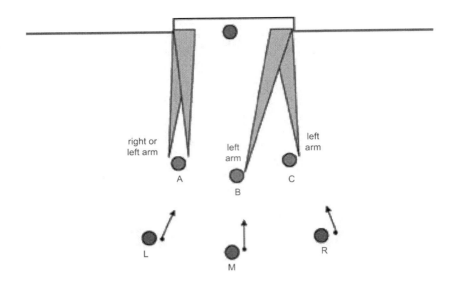

Scheme 9.4: Shooting past a block in a regular attacking set up (6 on 6)

3. Three players set in extra man positions, once on left side of attack, once on right side of attack. Two defenders sit on 2m in line with the two posts and attempt to block the shots. Third defender sits on 3m. The goalkeeper sits in a semi-vertical position with hands only slightly below the surface and ready for a quick intervention within his arm reach and short, fast slides across the goal. (Scheme 9.5a. and 9.5b).

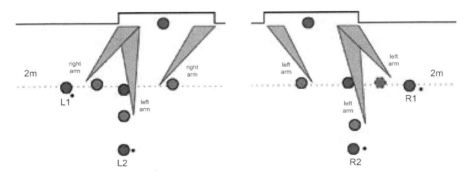

Scheme 9.5a and 9.5b: Shooting past a block in partly extra man attacking

4. Two players (L and R), set in partly extra man positions. Central defender sets on 2m positions. Another two defenders sit on 3m in line with the two posts and attempt to block the shots. Central defender blocks their shots with his right (shot from L) or with his left hand (shot from R). If the attacker R is left handed, he will be blocked with defender's right hand. (Scheme 9.6a).

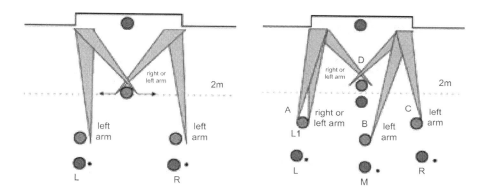

Scheme 9.6a and 9.6b: Shooting past a block in partly extra man and in a partly regular attacking

A group of three players set in their perimeter positions (R, M, L) in a partly regular attack with centre forward on 2m. Three defenders block their shots at an agreed distance. The defender on goalkeeper's right (A) blocks goalkeeper's right with his right (or left) hand while the defender on the other side (C) blocks with his left arm. The middle defender (B) blocks with his left arm most frequently. Centre back (D) blocks with his right (shot from L) or with his left hand (shot from R). (Scheme 9.6b).

10. GOALKEEPER IN A TEAM DEFENCE

The concept of "team defence" refers to a systematic, coordinated effort of field players and goalkeeper in preventing the opposite team to score a goal. It is a system in which roles and lines of movement of field players and the goalkeeper are determined and agreed to in accordance with the larger tactical play of the entire team during a game of water polo.

This "synthesis" of previous chapters looks at the organised actions of field players and the goalkeeper in regular (especially zone) and extra man defences. In both cases it is an absolute imperative for players and the goalkeeper to agree on and coordinate the defence in which every field player **blocks a part of the goal**. That is also the fundamental theoretical-tactical premise of this particular display of coordination between the defenders and the goalkeeper.

Naturally there is variety of individual and team tactics different from the ones shown in this book. By this I particularly mean the **"mirror image"**, type of **most frequently** blocking shots by defenders (defender block a right hand shot with his left arm). This type of blocking, for example is often used in outside positions, particularly by the middle defenders, or covering a cross-goal shot from the wings, leaving the goalkeeper to cover the close or "short" corner. The "mirror image" enables direct blocking of the ball but even the slightest move of the attacker outside the (predicted) shot line opens a much larger uncovered space between the goal posts. Blocking shots from the sides (wings) "mirror image" style, which commonly covers the diagonal, cross-goal shots and leaves the short corner to the goalkeeper, forces the goalkeeper to make a much longer move to adjust to the next possible shooter thus slowing down his reaction time.

All these variations are certainly allowed and possible because there is no ideal situation that applies universally across all kinds of players and goalkeepers. Each of these strategies has its benefits and pitfalls and a careful, close scrutiny of statistics might produce an optimal solution for a particular case.

Optimal blocking of space is important as it allows accurate identification of possible shooting "corridors" that the goalkeeper needs to cover. With the help of good blocking by his defenders, the goalkeeper can concentrate on a smaller area, which reduces his movement around the goal, increases the chances of stopping the shots and contributes to an overall greater effectiveness of the entire defence. Good and timely positioning by the goalkeeper not only increases his chances of stopping the ball but can often discourage the attacker from taking a (accurate) shot. Apart from that it gives the goalkeeper greater confidence and thus an advantage over the attackers. However, even in the best (blocking) defence the goalkeeper must not relax and drastically reduce his movements and jumps but instead use the opportunity to help the defenders when they are unable to act (eg. unable to block a shot or mark their player on time). If the goalkeeper does not help the defenders, the entire system loses its effectiveness and exposes larger deficiencies and mistakes.

I. Defending systems in regular (zone or combined press-zone) defence

1. The aim of the attacking team is to set in a semi circular position and this way opens an opportunity for a shot at goal. Defenders commonly defend by pressing the players on or close to the 2m line (first line), while the outside defenders (second line) defend the space between the attackers and the goal by blocking with one or two arms. (Scheme 10.1).

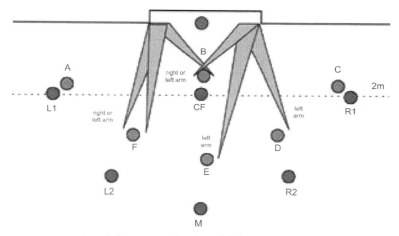

Scheme 10.1: Combined defence system

a. In a combined defence the first line defenders (A, B and C) do not allow very long cross passes between the two sides of attack, which immediately reduces the goalkeeper's movement between the posts.

b. The second line defenders (D, E and F) set up on approximately 4m to 5m away from the goal and defend the goal according to the agreed system. For example, D covers goalkeeper's left with his left arm (Picture 10.1), E defends the same corner where the ball came from, while F covers the goalkeeper's right with his right or left ("mirror image"), (also see Chapter 9., part 2.).

c. When the ball is passed from the right side of attack to the left (e.g. from R1 or R2 to M), the middle defender (E) raises his left arm to cover the goalkeeper's left corner. The attacker is left with the option of shooting through the middle or to the goalkeeper's right (see Scheme 10.1 and Picture 10.2). The same applies when the ball is passed from the left to the right side of attack.

85

Picture 10.1: Combined defence – R2 shooting, D blocking

Picture 10.2: Combined defence – M shooting (after receiving the ball from his right) E blocking (goalkeeper's left with his left arm)

Pictures 10.3a and 10.3b: Combined defence – L2 shooting, F blocking

   d. F blocks the short corner with his right (or left) arm, L2 is left with the option of shooting through the middle or diagonally, to the goalkeeper's left. (Picture 10.3a and 10.3b).

This type of defence reduces the goalkeeper's movement in goals as the short corners are "covered" by the defenders' arm block (L1 and R1 are pressed by A

87

and C defenders and unable to shoot comfortably) and as such increases his chances of successful defence.

Unpredictable situations may arise if the wings (L1 and R1) become free to receive the ball and/or have a shot. In such cases their closest defenders (A and C) block the short corner with their right (A) and left (C) arm. The outside defenders (F and D) can assist by extending their right (F) and left (D) arm to cover the short corner, leaving the goalkeeper shots through the middle and diagonally, cross-goal.

2. Attacking teams often use "screens" against a combined defence described above in order to improve their scoring chances. A "screen" is simply a move where one attacking player prevents the defender from directly attacking another attacker by positioning his body in the path of the defender. It usually requires two players, a blocker and receiver/shooter.

The example below (Scheme 10.2) shows how L2 commits his defender (F) by swimming towards the 2m line and then blocks the path of A who tries to mark L1. Attacker L1 is momentarily freed from pressing by A, receives the ball from another attacker (e.g. M at the point) and shoots or passes.

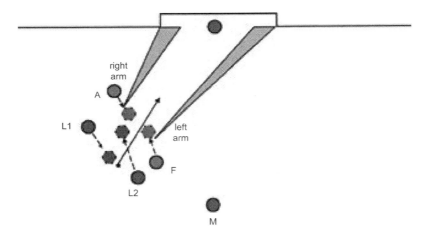

Scheme 10.2: Screen and blocking options

One possible defending/blocking solution in this situation is that A lifts his right arm (covering the short corner on goalkeeper's right) and F lifts his left arm to cover the cross-goal shot (goalkeeper's left). This leaves L1 only with a narrow shooting corridor between the two blocking defenders (as seen on the Picture 10.4 below), who face him straight on. Exactly the same applies on the opposite side except the defenders change the arms they block the shot with.

Picture 10.4: Blocking against a "screen" on the left side of attack

3. Teams with good goalkeepers frequently play combined or zone defence against teams of similar quality in order to threaten with an effective counterattack. As mentioned earlier, in this type of defence the engagement and coordination of all players and the goalkeeper is of paramount importance. When an attacker comes within the dangerous shot zone (approximately 5m to 7m from the goal) the defender's task is to "rush" the player as or before he shoots. After he prevents the immediate shooting danger, the defender returns back to his previous position or another appropriate position. As he repeats this action several times, the defender might lose the ideal blocking position or lift the wrong arm that disrupts the agreed coordination of blocking and defending between the players and the goalkeeper.

For example, when F blocks a shot by L2 with his right arm, L2 is forced to shoot to the middle or to the goalkeeper's left. His is also often unable to shoot a bounce shot because the centre forward and centre back occupy the area where the ball would ideally bounce. However, if F blocks in a "mirror image" style he opens the opportunity for L2 to move slightly to the left and shoot any kind of shot, including a bounce shot, to the short corner. In this case the defender blocks the area that is originally intended as goalkeeper's responsibility, while leaving a gap in the area he is responsible to block (short corner, narrow to the post). Scheme 10.3 below graphically shows these two concepts.

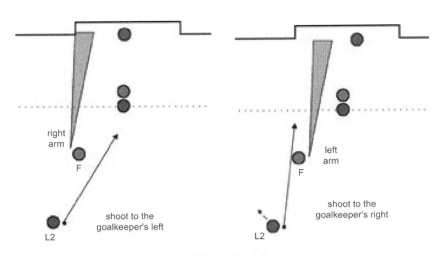

Scheme 10.3: Block with different arms

II. Defending systems in extra man defence

1. System 4-2 is probably the most commonly used system in extra man attack. We will use this system to illustrate several defending/blocking options available to players and goalkeepers in extra man defence. (Scheme 10.4). The **fundamental** premise remains that the **defenders block the short corner(s)** and leave the goalkeeper to defend the space within his arm reach in the middle of the goal.

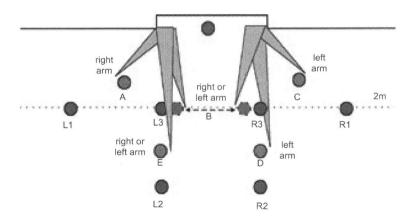

Scheme 10.4: System 4-2 extra man attack and basic blocking positions

a. When R1 has the ball, C moves slightly inside the 2m area and blocks the possible shooting lane to the short corner with his left arm. If R1 moves towards the outside positions, away from 2m, C adjusts his position to the

Picture 10.5: Extra man defence – ball at R1 (right handed)

right as he continues to cover the short corner with his left arm. In this case, the middle defender (B) may assist by blocking a possible diagonal, cross-goal shot by R1 with his left arm (if marking R3 at the time). (Picture 10.5).

When R1 is a left-hander the situation is more dangerous. As soon as the ball is passed to R1, C pushes off R3 (post player) into the 2m area to cut R1's shooting angle by a "mirror image" block (in this case he lifts his right arm). As soon as he recovers his legs from a side position into a vertical position he switches blocking arms and continues to block the short corner normally with his left arm. If R1 moves outward, away from the 2m line, C would lift right arms again, while B (middle defender) would attempt to block a shot to the goalkeeper's far right. The goalkeeper's responsibility remains the middle of the goal, which he ideally defends in a vertical position. He keeps both arms above the surface, ready to save a close range shot.

b. When the ball is at R2, D lifts his left arm and blocks goalkeeper's left corner near the post, B moves to his right and blocks the cross-goal shot with his left arm while leaning on L3 (post player). The system can be changed if the attacker is left handed (D lift right arm – "mirror image"). In this case the goalkeeper covers a narrow corridor within his arm reach. At this time the goalkeeper should be on approximately 0.5m to 0.7m in front of the goal line in a semi-vertical position with his hands very shallow to enable a quick reaction (see Picture 10.6).

Picture 10.6: Extra man defence – ball at R2

c. When the ball is at L2, the same blocking rules as in b. apply, except the sides and arms are now switched. E blocks goalkeeper's right with his right (or left – "mirror image") arm while B in the middle moves across to lean on R3 to cover a cross-goal shot with his right arm. The goalkeeper is left with the responsibility for the corridor of the same width (arm's reach) while waiting for a shot in a semi vertical position approximately 0.5m to 0.7m in front of the goal line (see Pictures 10.7a and 10.7b).

d. When the ball is passed to L1, A pushes off L3 (post) with his left arm to immediately cut L1's shooting angle. He moves on an angle inside 2m and towards the shooter while blocking "mirror image" style. As soon as he regains a vertical position with his legs underneath him, he continues to block the short corner (in this case the goalkeeper's right, near the post) with his right arm. (Picture 10.8). If L1 moves towards the outside positions, away from 2m line, in order to improve his shooting angle, A should lift his left arm ("mirror image") again as well and block the short corner. In this case the middle defender helps the goalkeeper by defending a possible cross-goal shot with his right arm. The goalkeeper sits in a vertical position with both arms above his head, ready to cover the area near his body and above his head.

2. In a most common scenario of defence against a 3-3 extra man attack, the defenders on 2m line (A, B and C) are responsible for one player each, but are

Picture 10.7a and 10.7b: Extra man defence – ball at L2

Picture 10.8: Extra man defence – ball at L1

still able to help with the blocking. The two outside defenders (D and E) **shuffle** between the three outside attackers (R2, M and L2) and try to prevent them from making accurate passes or quality shots. (Scheme 10.5).

As far as blocking is concerned, when the ball is at R2, C splits a little from the R1 and tries to block the goalkeeper's left corner with his right arm, while B blocks goalkeeper's right corner. The most probable shot in this situation would be to the middle or the goalkeeper's right.

The same applies on the other side with arms and corners reversed (ball at L2, A blocks the goalkeeper's right corner with his left arm, B blocks the cross-goal shot to the goalkeeper's left). The most probable shot would be to the middle or the goalkeeper's left. In both cases, the blocking defenders try to "channel" the probable shot towards the middle, where the goalkeeper sits in a semi vertical position with his hands shallow and ready for a quick intervention.

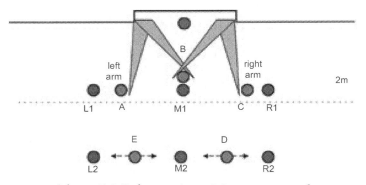

Scheme 10.5: Defence against a 3-3 extra man attack

94

3. Within the 4-2 extra man defence system, teams sometimes apply a type of defence, popularly called "the house" in Croatia. (Scheme 10.6). In this system, A and C defenders come back towards the goal and lift both (**new rules: one**) arm(s) virtually on the goal line near the posts on each side of the goal. The goalkeeper is positioned slightly in front of the goal line and, like the two defenders on the goal line, with his two arms and his body lifted high. B shuffles intensely between L3 and R3 posts while D shuffles between R1 and R2 and lifts his left arm to cover the goalkeeper's left corner when the ball is at R2. The same applies to E who shuffles between L2 and L1 and blocks the goalkeeper's right with his right (or left) arm when the ball is at L2. (Picture 10.9).

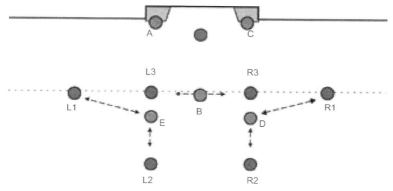

Scheme 10.6: "The house", 4-2 extra man defence variation

Picture 10.9: "The house", 4-2 extra man defence variation

11. OTHER GOALKEEPING EXERCISES

This chapter covers several exercises that may appear relatively minor to the rest of the goalkeeping practice, as they are often even overlooked in games and training. However, any of these elements may often become crucial to the outcome of a game.

We have mentioned that the goalkeeper is also the first attacker of the team, particularly in situations when he stops a shot and regains possession of the ball. The level of his alertness, speed of reaction, tactical maturity timely noticing of an attacking opportunity and accurate passing directly affects the quality of the team's attack. He is even allowed a direct shot at the opposition goal, which further increases his role in the game, although such shots are rarely possible and/or successful.

Two exercises we would like to pay particular attention to, due to their importance in a game, are steals and accurate long distance passing.

- **Steals by swimming and turning**

  Following the basic instructions for starting at the ball in Chapter 5., this exercise is most effectively done while training a regular (6 on 6) defence. As the ball is passed to the CF (centre forwards), or even while the CF is in possession of it, the goalkeeper starts a fast, powerful and very short swim to steal the ball with a strong, asymmetrical eggbeater kick. The success of the intervention greatly depends on the goalkeeper's judgement of the distance to the ball and his timely reaction. Ideally, the goalkeeper initiates the move as the ball flies towards the CF and when the CF is not in control of it. The goalkeeper should not be too far from the CF and the entire move must be coordinated with the CB (centre backs). In case of a bad judgement, the goalkeeper should immediately stop, sit in a high position and get ready for a jump while anticipating a shot from the CF.

- **Long distance passing**

  When and where to pass the ball to an attacking player is a matter of skill, experience and tactical maturity of a goalkeeper. In a group counter attack, the goalkeeper usually passes to the right side, on the hand or in the vicinity, usually in front, of the attacking player, depending on the position of the defender(s). In an individual counter attack, the goalkeeper most frequently passes the ball in front of the advancing attacker.

  To ensure the pass is always safe, accurate and timely, the goalkeeper may swim several strokes forward to shorten the distance and increase accuracy of a pass, stop and lift the ball high in one hand to allow for his teammates to see it. He supports the high vertical body position with powerful sculling with his opposite arm. As an opportunity arises he throws an appropriate pass. If the goalkeeper is unsure about the success of the pass before he throws it, it is better for him to wait for a safer option and not give away the ball possession by a bad pass. Notably, goalkeeper's passing mistakes are often penalised by a goal.

Long distance passing can be practiced well, particularly during the team or individual counter-attack training.

- **Various other exercises**

1. *Protecting the ball (with both hands)* – This is a commonly used element of the game when the goalkeeper is under direct physical pressure by an attacker. Having gained possession of the ball with both hands, the goalkeeper quickly turns his back to the opposition player and protects the ball with his body. With a powerful kick he quickly starts swimming away from the player. In a hopeless situation with no support from his teammates he throws the ball over the line in the corner.

2. *Deliberate leaving of space when stopping shots ("leading on")* – Goalkeeper can often leave a part of his goal seemingly uncovered (or move slightly further forward) moments before an attacker takes a shot. This can lead to the attacker shooting to the side of the goal that looks free but the goalkeeper anticipates the shot to go exactly there as he jumps to save it. Similarly to the straight shots to one side of the goal, the tactic can be applied to lob shots. The goalkeeper moves slightly forward, leaving the player with an impression that a lob shot is the best scoring option. As he shoots a lob, the goalkeeper retreats and stops the ball. A "lead on" can be particularly effective against weaker and inexperienced shooters.

3. *"Leading on" at penalty shots* – The basic technique for stopping a penalty shot is discussed in Chapter 5. In addition to that, the goalkeeper can lean, after the initial "opening" forwards, to a side he had previously chosen to jump to. In another variation of penalty stopping, he can position himself more to one side of the goal, thus leaving the other side temptingly open for the shooter. As the referee whistles, he stretches to the "open" side to try and stop the ball.

12. (PRE)GAME REMARKS

In the introduction to this book we have noted the importance of a goalkeeper in water polo and his role as one of the most responsible and important in the entire team. The goalkeeper is the corrector of all mistakes made by the field players. But as much as the individual styles and tactics of each goalkeeper differ there are certain elements that are common to all goalkeepers and which directly determine the quality of a goalkeeper.

The most important common element is the ability to hold concentration for long periods of time. A good goalkeeper follows the play anywhere in the field fully concentrated and, of course, particularly when the team is defending. In this context, concentration is the ability to maintain focus without interruption during the course of an entire game. Maintenance of good concentration requires good physical fitness.

The goalkeeper must quickly notice, and ideally anticipate, any changes during the game that may affect his intervention. As a rule he must "follow the ball" at all times and set his body position according to the position of the ball. However, there are exemptions to this rule. The goalkeeper can neglect a player with the ball who has no intention or ability to throw a direct shot at and positions himself according to the more dangerous player(s) who are likely to receive a pass and continue the play. This is particularly important in situations inside the 7m area. When the CF has a free throw, the goalkeeper must position himself according to the player who is most likely to receive the pass or shoot and not according to the CF. Similarly, if any player other than CF plays the ball from a free throw inside 7m, the goalkeeper can position himself according to the CF to increase the chance of a steal.

From this element follows the next important element of goalkeeping - the correct choice of situational and body position in goals. This is a crucial factor that directly determines the success of goalkeeping and provides information on goalkeeper's technical and tactical ability and quality. The goalkeeper must constantly control his position and movement in relation to the posts and try to equally cover the entire goal and/ or the space where the shot is expected to. It is very important for the goalkeeper to position his body directly to the shooter, most often with short and fast glides around the goal. As he moves across he should wait with his jump slightly, but only enough to judge the situation and react according to the play.

Jumping must be fast and short to the side with maximal leg support and less arm support with an appropriate leaning of the body (less horizontal position preferred). While a player is baulking the goalkeeper should stay ready but calm and not allow any significant breaking of his basic position by sudden jerks and lifts of his body, which inevitably result in a loss of basic position and often a slower reaction.

During the game, the goalkeeper should cooperate with the field players and coordinate the defence but not to the point of distraction and detriment or neglect of his primary duties in the goal. When he gains possession of the ball, either after a save or at goal throw, the goalkeeper must execute a simple, timely and accurate pass to his team mates in attack.

In a systematic defence, the goalkeeper should concentrate maximally on the part of the goal he is directly responsible but with a "reserve" to save any shots the defenders may let through by poor blocking of their corridors. Attackers may often move to destabilise defenders' blocking and open up a shooting angle where the goalkeeper must intervene to prevent a goal. The goalkeeper must also be ready for any sudden, surprise shots, particularly at the start of the opposition's attack.

Before the game the goalkeeper must "scout" the opposition and establish their preferred shooting styles and favourite shooting corners. He must also familiarise himself with the opposition's overall attacking tactics and the most frequent ways of ending their attacks. The goalkeeper must also find ways of relaxation and off-loading of pre-game pressure and possible performance anxiety that could adversely affect him and lead to a nervous game with little confidence.

The goalkeeper should start his game warm up on land with components of callisthenics and stretching. After a short swimming warm up, he should warm the legs, followed by basic jumping exercises and very short sprints. As he stands in the goal, he should request a series of fast shots with no baulks, directed within his arm reach. After that the goalkeeper should request a variety of shots by field players. The shooting must increase the intensity towards the start of the game. After a brief rest period and just before the start of the game, the goalkeeper directs the players to shoot few more fast shots in order to get him ready for the start. It is very important that the goalkeeper is fully ready at the start of the game as the initial few saves provide confidence for him and his team.

Finally, the coach must know the goalkeeper's psychological attributes as a part of the overall readiness of the goalkeeper to play successfully. This particularly relates to his intellectual, emotional and motivational state and his behaviour as a team member. The coach must know if the goalkeeper's physical and psychological attributes are stable enough to ensure effective goalkeeping and adaptation in unique, often stressful situations that occur during games. The goalkeeper should be particularly well motivated, have the ability to initiate action and function well and in coordination within a group. It is well known that a homogeneous team achieves better working and sporting results.

13. STATISTICS

New developments in statistical analysis of individual players and teams in recent years have been greatly justifiable and welcome. Of course, it is not always easy to judge and analyse individual and team technical-tactical abilities. A useful repertoire of the (most) important and easily measurable elements of a water polo game can provide a good idea of effectiveness and impact of particular players or teams. As the team consists of a set of individual players and their individual tactics and abilities their analysis can lead to an accurate overall team analysis.

The presented example is a very basic example how simple and easily measurable elements of the game can derive a lot of useful information for analysis of a particular player or a team.

The data was entered through a very simple tabular form on a computer, which covers some of the most important parameters of individual players. This way we could analyse the data against the tactics employed by both teams and easily determine the effect of individual players in the game. Naturally, subjective judgements by the coach are an integral part of the overall analysis, complemented by the statistics.

After a series of games, we can compare effectiveness of players of all team members, identify trends and average the effectiveness of the selected elements in a team game (eg. average extra man attack conversion, extra man defence, goalkeeper saves etc.).

The example shown in this book is simply that - an example. It allows for addition of a range of other elements in order to improve the analysis by the coach. For practical purposes, we opted for the fastest and simplest ways of entering data during the game while the synthesis after the game provided a great deal of useful information. This points out to the tendency to standardise the forms and ways of entering statistical data.

Competition   Place   Date

Results: TeamA - TeamB/TeamA - TeamC/TeamA - TeamD/TeamA - TeamE/TeamF/TeamA - TeamG/TeamA - TeamH/TeamA - TeamI

Team A

Players Team A	Shots num.par	Scored num.par	Shots play.more	Scored play.more	Shots count.at	Scored count.at	Provoked penalty	Shots penalty	Scored penalty	Centrefw. passed	Provoked exclusion	Centrefw. efficiency	Shot saved num.parity	Shot saved player les	Total Goals	Shots saved %
Goalkeeper	0	0									0		56	16	59	55%
Player 1	24	8	8	4	0	0	0	0	0		0					
Player 2	16	8	16	16	0	0	0	0	0		16					
Player 3	32	8	16	8	0	0	0	0	0		16					
Player 4	0	0	0	0	0	0	8	8	7		8					
Centre forw.	16	8	8	8	0	0	8	0	0	48	22	75%				
Player 5	0	0	0	0	8	8	6	0	0		8					
Player 6	16	8	24	16	0	0	0	0	0		0					
Centre forw.	16	8	0	0	0	0	6	0	0	33	9	70%				
Player 7	0	0	0	0	16	8	0	0	0		0					
Player 8	24	8	16	4	0	0	0	0	0		8					
Player 9	0	0	0	0	0	0	0	0	0		0					
Goalkeeper	0	0									0		64	46	41	66%
TOTAL	144	56	88	56	24	16	20	8	7	81	87		120	32	100	152
%		39%		64%		67%			88%			73%				60%

Wining balls	64
Loosing balls	32

Player less	Saved	%
64	32	50%

Notice:

Team A

Shots with numerical parity

Position	Shots	Scored	%
Left wing	24	8	33%
Left side	16	8	50%
Centre side	32	8	25%
Right side	16	8	50%
Right wing	24	8	33%
Sub Total	**112**	**40**	**36%**
Centre forw.	32	16	50%
TOTAL	**144**	**56**	**39%**

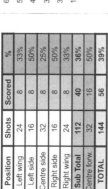

Shots with player more

Position	Shots	Scored	%
Left wing	8	4	50%
Left side	16	16	100%
Right side	16	8	50%
Left 2m	8	8	100%
Right 2m	24	16	67%
	16	4	25%
TOTAL	**88**	**56**	**64%**

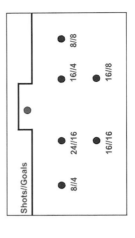

GOAL KEEPER'S SAVES

Goalkeeper's saves	Saves num. parity	Goals num. parity	% Saves num. parity	Saves player less	Goals player less	% Saves player less
Total	120	68	36%	32	32	50%

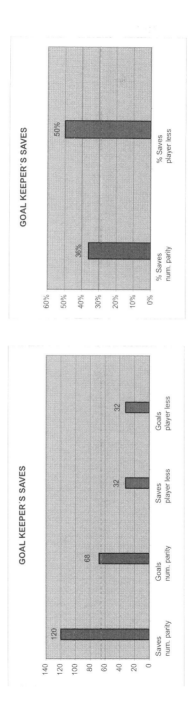

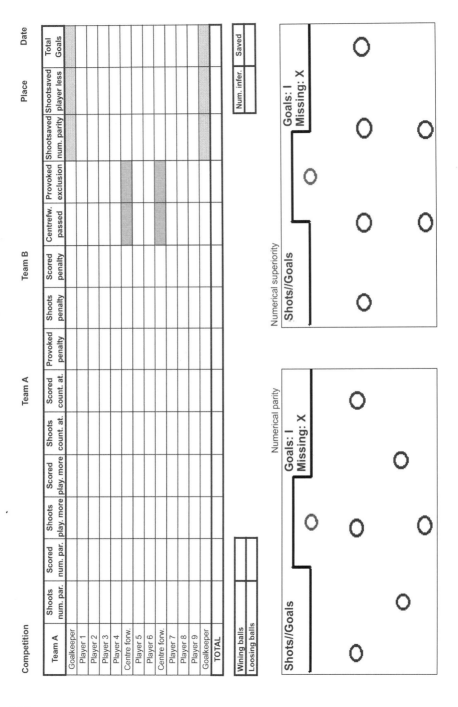

14. GLOSSARY OF TERMS

The Glossary contains several terms that are used in different countries but essentially mean the same.

A

Arm reach – The extent of fully outstretched arms in a horizontal position at shoulder height away from the body.

B

Basic goalkeeping position – Detailed description in Chapter 4.

Backhand, scoop, pull on – types of shots commonly used by centre forwards of post players (close range shots; see Chapter 5.).

Baulking – (also "faking", "lifting", "locking") – A simulated shot movement with the aim of destabilising the defence (see Chapter 5.).

Bounce shot (also "skip shots") – Bouncing the ball off the water surface (see Chapter 5.).

Butterfly – In this book butterfly is assumed to be exclusively with a breastroke kick.

C

Centre forwards (CF) – (also "hole", "anchor", "pivot"). Central attacking position approximately on 2m line.

Centre backs (CB) – (also "back", "central"). Marking the CB.

Commit – (also "lock the goalie") to convince the defence of a certain shot or a scoring opportunity, usually with effective use of space and good baulking.

Cross-goal – (also "cross cage", "diagonal", "long corner") – Shots to the "long" corner, farthest to the shooter (Chapter 7.).

D

Drivers – (also "flats", "left/right outsider") – Side positions on the outside perimeter of the attack.

E

Eggbeater – (also "bicycle") – Powerful and most commonly used kicking technique for treading water in water polo. Consists of series of interchangeable kicks with both legs.

Exercises – (also "drills") – Smaller, structured parts of a training session designed to enhance a particular skill or ability.

105

H

Hook out – Attacker swims on a short angle, usually towards the edge of the field, in order to receive the ball form another player or goalkeeper. Commonly used in counterattack (transition).

J

Jump – (also known as "explosion") – Quick propulsion of the body out of the water.

L

Lateral movement – gliding and skimming (see Chapter 4. for a detailed description), term "lateral movement" used further in text – both gliding and skimming can be used.

Leading arm (hand) – The arm that moves towards the ball (counter is the "opposite arm" or "pushing arm; see Chapter 4.).

Leading on – To leave a part of the goal seemingly uncovered but entice and anticipate a shot in that particular corner (see Chapter 11.).

M

Mirror image blocking – If faced straight, attacker's shot is blocked by the defender with the opposite arm (eg. right handed shooter blocked with defender's left hand and vice versa).

O

Off hand shot – Quick shots with no baulking (see Chapter 7.).

P

Pick – Similar to screen, attackers use short swimming on a sharp angle in order to advance ahead of the defender (see Chapter 8.).

Post – (also "upright") – Commonly attackers L3 and R3 in "6 on 5" play who stay relatively close in line with the goalpost.

Probable shot zone – The most frequent distance of shots at goal (see Chapter 7.).

R

Ready Position – Goalkeeper's high position with hands in the water, usually just before a jump.

Rush – Usually a short, very fast swim or horizontal jump of a defender toward an attacker (see Chapter 10.).

S

Scout – To make notes about opposition players and their particular technical, tactical abilities and preferences (see Chapter 12.).

Screen – Attacking player prevents defender from directly attacking another attacker by positioning his body in the path of the defender. It usually requires two players, a blocker and receiver/ shooter (see Chapter 8.).

Sculling – Semi circular movement of hands (see Chapter 4.).

Short corner – The corner closest to the shooter (see Chapter 7.).

Shuffle – Similar to rush, the aim is usually to slow down the movement of an attacker with a direct movement towards him or to a particular space that needs to be defended.

"Slow-fast" – (also "delay", "hold", "lazy" shots) – After a pause or slowing of the arm movement during a shot the ball is thrown relatively faster and usually with a good wrist snap (see Chapter 8.).

W

Walking – Water polo eggbeater kick in a vertical body position (see Chapter 4.)

Wing – The extreme attacking positions (left/right) on approximately 2m line (see Chapter 7.).

15. BIBLIOGRAPHY

1. **Banđur:** *Trening golmana, 1975*
2. **FINA:** Water Polo Manual, 1990
3. **Lozovina:** *Suvremena taktika vaterpolo igre, 1970*
4. **Lozovina:** *Karakteristike vaterpolista u morfološkom prostoru, 1981*
5. **Lozovina:** *Utjecaj morfoloških karakteristika i motoričkih sposobnosti u plivanju na uspješnost igrača u vaterpolu, 1983*
6. **Lozovina:** *Kretanje igrača u vaterpolu i trenažni postupci za razvoj energetskih potencijala, 1984*
7. **Lozovina:** *Vaterpolo – tehnika, taktika i vratar u vaterpolu, 1995*
8. **Lozovina:** *Jednadžba specifikacije sportske aktivnosti, 1996*
9. **Pavičić, Šimenc, Lozovina:** *Analiza repertoara elemenata vaterpolo tehnike, 1988*
10. **Rossi:** *Golman – pojam, osnovi i tehnika obrane gola, Vaterpolo, 1984*
11. **Rossi:** *Postavljanje golmana "na golu" i osnovni načini obrane, 1984*
12. **Šimenc:** *Napad i obrana s igračem više i s igračem manje, 1973*
13. **Ušakov, Rižak, Šteler :** Водное Поло, 1963

110

CROATIAN OLYMPIC COMMITTEE   SPLIT SPORT FEDERATION   SPLIT-DALMATIAN COUNTY
Administrative division for education, culture and sports

Energy path to your home was our slogan, with which we have been realizing our mission in the domestic and the international market during the past fifty-five years, from the foundation of the company in 1949. until today, and we have been carrying out many business operations in the field of the project, the production and the construction of electro-energetic objects, objects of road, railway and city traffic, of telecommunications infrastructure for all purposes, as well as the illumination of sports and other objects. Today, it is safe when we say that it was the The path of positive energy.

THE PATH OF POSITIVE ENERGY

Electric Power Company for Design, Production and Construction
www.dalekovod.com

Made in the USA
San Bernardino, CA
12 December 2016